FOOTPATHS OF BRITAIN

NORTH-EAST
ENGLAND

p

This is a Parragon Book
First published in 2003

Parragon
Queen Street House
4 Queen Street
Bath BA1 1HE
United Kingdom

Created and produced by
The Bridgewater Book Company Ltd,
Lewes, East Sussex

ISBN: 1-40540-503-1

Printed in China

www.walkingworld.com

Visit the Walkingworld website at
www.walkingworld.com

All the walks in this book are available in more
detailed form on the Walkingworld website.
The route instructions have photographs at key
decision points to help you to navigate, and
each walk comes with an Ordnance Survey®
map. Simply print them out on A4 paper
and you are ready to go! A modest annual
subscription gives you access to over 1,400
walks, all in this easy-to-follow format. If you
wish, you can purchase individual walks for a
small fee.

Next to every walk in this book you will see
a Walk ID. You can enter this ID number on
Walkingworld's 'Find a Walk' page and you will
be taken straight to the details of that walk.

CONTENTS

Introduction

Britain is a fabulous place to walk. We are blessed with a varied and beautiful landscape, a dense network of public footpaths and places of historical interest at every corner. Add to all this the many thousands of well-placed pubs, tea shops and visitor attractions, and it's easy to see why walking is a treasured pastime for millions of people.

Walking is the perfect way to keep fit and healthy. It is good for your heart, muscles and body generally, without making the extreme demands of many sports. For most walkers, however, the health benefits are secondary. We walk for the sheer pleasure of it – being able to breathe in the fresh air, enjoy the company of our friends and 'get away from it all'.

Equipment

If you take up walking as a hobby, it is quite possible to spend a fortune on specialist outdoor kit. But you really don't need to. Just invest in a few inexpensive basics and you'll be ready to enjoy any of the walks in this book.

For footwear, boots are definitely best as they provide you with ankle support and protection from the inevitable mud, nettles and puddles. A lightweight pair should be fine if you have no intention of venturing up big hills or over rugged terrain. If you are not sure what to get, go to a specialist shop and ask for advice. Above all, choose boots that fit well and are comfortable.

Take clothing to deal with any weather that you may encounter. Allow for the 'wind-chill' factor – if your clothes get wet you will feel this cooling effect even more. Carry a small rucksack with a spare top, a hat and waterproofs, just in case. The key is being able to put on and take off layers of clothing at will and so keep an even, comfortable temperature throughout the day.

It's a good idea to carry some food and drink. Walking is exercise and you need to replace the fluid you lose through perspiration. Take a bottle of soft drink or water, and sip it regularly rather than downing it in one go. The occasional chocolate bar, sandwich or biscuit can work wonders when energy levels are flagging.

Walking poles – the modern version of the walking stick – are worth considering. They help you to balance and allow your arms to take some of the strain when going uphill. They also lessen the impact on your knees on downhill slopes. Don't be fooled into thinking that poles are just for the older walker – they are popular with trekkers and mountaineers of all ages.

Finding your way

Most walkers use Ordnance Survey® maps, rightly considered to be among the most accurate, up-to-date and 'walker–friendly' in the world. The 1:50,000 scale Landranger series has long been a favourite of outdoor enthusiasts. Almost all areas of Britain are also covered by the more detailed 1:25,000 scale Explorer and Explorer OL series. These include features such as field boundaries, farm buildings and small streams.

Having a map and compass – and learning how to use them – is vital to being safe in the countryside. Compass and map skills come with practice – there is no substitute for taking them out and having a go. Buy a compass with a transparent base plate and rotating dial; you will find this type in any outdoor shop. Most come with simple instructions – if not, ask in the shop for a guide.

If this all sounds a bit serious, I urge you not to worry too much about getting lost. We have all done it – some of us more often than we care to admit! You are unlikely to come to much harm unless you are on a featureless hilltop or out in very poor weather. If you want to build up your confidence, start with shorter routes through farmland or along the coastline and allow yourself plenty of time.

key to maps

Symbol	Description	Symbol	Description
	Telephone		Lighthouse
	Start of walk		Camping
	Viewpoint	▲	Youth hostel
	Pylon		Bridge
	Triangulation point		Windmill
	Radio mast		Highest point/summit
	Church with Steeple	PH	Public house
	Church without Steeple	PC	Public convenience
	Chapel	1666	Place of historical interest
	Power lines		Embankment/cutting
	Golf course		Rocky area/ sharp drop
	Picnic area		Building
	Car park		Castle
	Information	☆	Tumulus
			Garden

There are plenty of walks in this book that are perfect for the beginner. You can make navigating even easier by downloading the routes in this book from Walkingworld's website: www.walkingworld.com. These detailed walk instructions feature a photograph at each major decision point, to help you confirm your position and see where to go next.

Another alternative is to join a local walking group

Marsh		Lake/sea	
Railway + station			
Dismantled railway		Woods	
Route of walk		Sand	
A Road			
B Road		Dunes	
Footpath		Urban	
Track/unclassified road			
Stream			
River			
Large river/estuary			

0   1 km   1 mile

Difficulty Rating

Gentle Stroll   Moderate Walk

Easy Walk   Hill Scramble

Time

Each circle = 1 hour

Half circle = ½ hour

and learn from others. There are hundreds of such groups around the country, with members keen to share their experience and skills.

Enough words. Take the walks in this book as your inspiration. Grab your map and compass, and put on your boots. It's time to go out and walk!

Have fun.

DAVID STEWART *Walkingworld*

▲ Map: Explorer 332	Difficulty rating	Time	▲ Lake, Sea, Pub, Woodland, Wildlife, Great views
▲ Distance: 9.66 km/6 miles			
▲ Walk ID: 1498 Julia Ewart			

Howick Hall from Boulmer

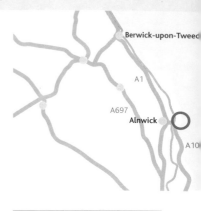

This walk takes you from the fishing village of Boulmer, along the coastal path and into the wood of the Howick Estate, before rejoining the outward track back along the coast to Boulmer.

❶ From the car park, head north along a track to join the footpath alongside the road. Continue ahead past the Fishing Boat pub.

❷ At the junction, leave the main road and follow the No Through Road. Follow the rough stone track through a series of gates and on to the beach. Turn left, continuing over a bridge and through another gate. Follow the track through the field and past a parking area. The track continues alongside the beach, rising over the dunes. Go through the next gate and cross the bridge.

❸ Turn left away from the beach and head along a grass track into the wood. Continue on the track labelled 'Long Walk'. Go through a turnstile, keeping left. The stoned track meets a grassed track going left. Follow this track as it bears left over a small bridge and continues alongside the stream.

❹ At the end of the 'Long Walk' go through the gate on to the main road. Turn right and pass the entrance of Howick Hall. Follow the road round a right hand bend, past another gate out of the woods on your right and a turning to Howick village on your left. Continue to the corner, with the sea in front of you.

❺ Take the footpath towards the sea. Go through the gate and turn right, heading along the top of the dunes. Follow the track over three stiles, then past four marker posts. Cross the next stile and the bridge that you crossed earlier. Go through the gate and along the top footpath.

❻ Go through the next gate and cross the bridge. Go through the gate to your right and continue back along the outward track to the car park.

further information

The 'Long Walk' is closed on the second Wednesday of February each year, as it is not a public footpath.

access information

Take the A1 to Alnwick, then from Alnwick take the A1068 out signposted Boulmer, Alnmouth, Warkworth, Amble. At Lesbury turn left at the junction before the bridge, signed Boulmer. Continue on this road until you reach the village, parking in the car park on the right-hand side, on the dunes.

From seashore through woodland to grassy meadows, there is a wonderful variety of landscapes on this walk.

Howick

Howick
Hall

Gardens

4

5

Rumbling
Kern

3

6

Sugar Sands

Howdiemount Sands

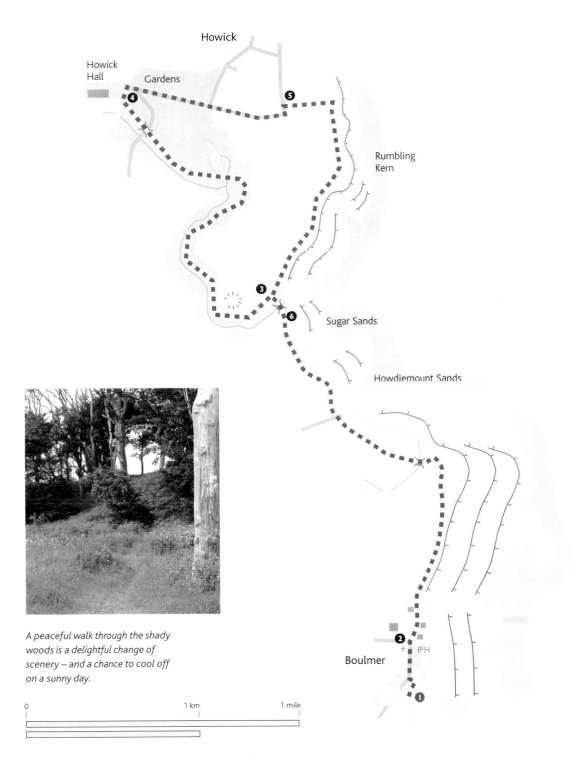

A peaceful walk through the shady
woods is a delightful change of
scenery – and a chance to cool off
on a sunny day.

2

✝ PH

Boulmer

1

0   1 km   1 mile

▲ Map: Explorer 340
▲ Distance: 16 km/10 miles
▲ Walk ID: 507 H. Weightman

Difficulty rating

👣👣

Time

●●●●◖

▲ Pub, Church, Castle, Birds, Great Views

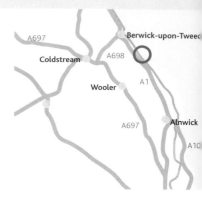

Holy Island from Beal Sands

This walk crosses the vast Goswick Sands to reach Holy Island by The Snook, then continues to the village and castle to return by the Pilgrim's Way. Before you start, be sure to note the information about tides and observe the warnings.

❶ From the parking area, follow the footpath, skirting Beal Point to enter the estuary. Cross the dyke, turn right and pass over the sluice-bridge, before continuing along a raised track towards the prominent tower by Beachcomber Farm. At the tower, turn right and head through the dunes to the beach. Walk for 600 m towards the shoreline.

❷ Turn diagonally right and cross the sands to Lindisfarne, heading towards a small tower (The Snook). After about 1 km wade across the watercourse, or follow the bank for 200 m for an easier crossing.

❸ At the Snook, check the time – it should have taken no more than 2 hours to reach this point. Pass to the left of the farm buildings and continue down the track to meet the causeway. Turn left to reach the village. Just past the sign to the Lindisfarne Hotel turn left and head towards the harbour.

❹ At the harbour, take in the fine views of the castle, the Farne Islands and Bamburgh. Follow the path to the castle. After visiting the castle, return to the shore. Climb by the path to the left and follow it left around a field border.

❺ Turn left at the signpost, following the path back to the village. Retrace your steps to reach the causeway.

❻ This is the start of The Pilgrims' Way. Do not attempt this crossing less than

3 hours before the end of safe crossing time posted on the tide tables. Follow the line of the poles if conditions are right, or follow the causeway, remembering that this, too, will be impassable after the safe crossing time. Both routes end at the start point of this walk.

access information

Road access is signed from the A1 south of Berwick-upon-Tweed. There is no public transport to the island.

further information

IMPORTANT: This walk involves two crossings of tidal areas that are submerged to a depth of 2 m at high tide. The most comprehensive tide information is available from www.northumberland.gov.uk/vg/tidetabl.html.

Along the coast from Holy Island, Bamburgh Castle stands on an ancient rocky outcrop overlooking kilometres of beautiful sandy beach.

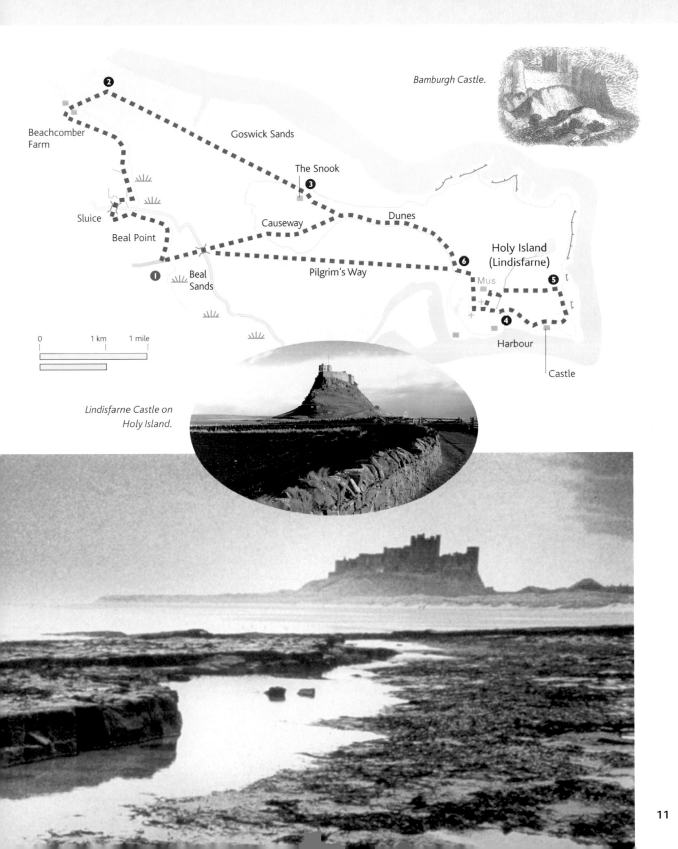

Bamburgh Castle.

2

Beachcomber
Farm

Goswick Sands

The Snook
3

Sluice

Causeway

Dunes

Beal Point

Holy Island
(Lindisfarne)

6

Mus

1

Beal
Sands

Pilgrim's Way

5

0   1 km   1 mile

4

Harbour

Castle

Lindisfarne Castle on
Holy Island.

▲ Map: Explorer 339
▲ Distance: 16 km/10 miles
▲ Walk ID: 509 H. Weightman

Difficulty rating

👣👣👣

Time

●●●●◗

▲ River, Sea, Pub, Church, Castle,
Wildlife, Birds, Flowers, Food Shop,
Tea Shop, Ancient Monument

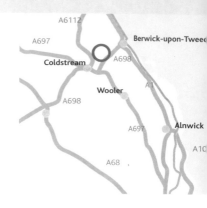

Tweed Walkway: Berwick from Norham

Starting at Norham Bridge, this linear walk passes Norham Castle and meanders along the river bank, passing one of the oldest suspension bridges in the country, to reach Berwick-upon-Tweed.

❶ The walk begins on the southern side of Norham Bridge. Climb over the wall, go down the steps to the River Tweed and follow the river bank round. Cross a footbridge, with Norham Castle directly ahead of you. Follow the path through the woods to the north of the castle.

❷ Leave the river bank and cross the stile. Follow the path, climbing gently through fields to enter a small wood. Turn left downhill at the signpost for Horncliffe.

❸ At Horncliffe, turn right at the T-junction and continue to the main street. Turn left to take the small road next to The Fisher's Arms.

❹ Bear left and follow the track, then the path, back down to the river bank. Continue along the bank for 1 km. The road swings left over the Chainbridge suspension bridge and into Scotland. Continue straight ahead past a house and through a gate to return to the river bank. The road leads to West Ord Farm — bear slightly left and cross a stile to continue on the river bank.

❺ Climb the steps through the thickets to cross a waymarked stile. Follow the field boundary to the left. Cross the A1 trunk road through a break in the hedgerow, making for the playground and picnic area. Go left behind the brightly painted play structure and then ahead for 50 m.

❻ Cross the stile and follow a path that dips to river-level, before climbing through woods to reach open fields. Bear left at the track junction and pass through a waymarked gate next to Berwick's sewage works. Follow the track around the plant and continue along the river. Passing under the railway bridge, bear slightly left towards Berwick.

❼ Turn left over Berwick Old Bridge to enter the town by Bridge Street.

access information

Buses run from Golden Square in Berwick-upon-Tweed to Norham. Berwick itself is on the A1, and is served by frequent trains, on the main Edinburgh to London east-coast line.

This walk takes you through woods and fields along the southern bank of the meandering River Tweed.

Berwick is the most northern town in England, and stands at the mouth of the River Tweed.

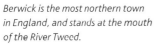

Berwick

A1

⑤

⑥

Chainbridge
suspension
bridge

West Ord
Farm

River Tweed

④

PH ✝

③ Horncliffe

②

Norham Castle, built of pink sandstone, is the subject of many paintings.

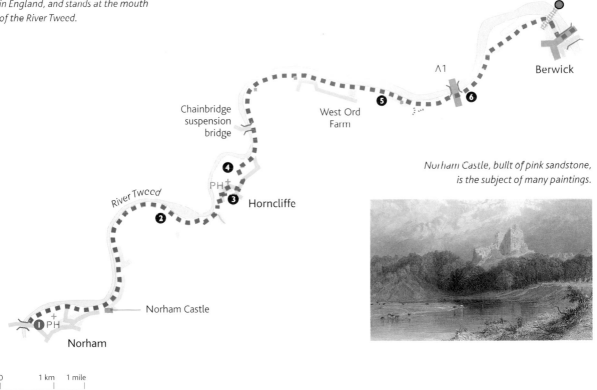

Norham Castle

① PH ✝

Norham

0   1 km   1 mile

▲ Map: Explorer OL 43

▲ Distance: 6 km/3¾ miles

▲ Walk ID: 1179 Jim Lowery

Difficulty rating

Time

▲ River, Pub, Wildlife, Birds, Good for Kids, Mostly Flat, Public Transport, Woodland

River North Tyne from Acomb

This is a pleasant figure-of-eight walk with good stretches along the riverside, making it ideal for picnics and bathing on warm summer days. The return route follows the old railway line.

❶ Start from the lay-by at the junction of the A69 and A6079. Follow the A6079 along the footpath on the right-hand side of the road. Turn left at the junction towards Acomb Industrial Estate. Follow the road, passing a junction to a farm on the right.

❷ At the next track junction, continue under the arch and through a gate, gently downhill towards the river, where the North and South Tyne meet. Turn right on to a track along the North Tyne.

❸ Follow a wider track a little further from the river and pass a fence, continuing as the path narrows. The river has some rapids here. Continue following the track, which soon begins to meander through a wide, steep-sided gorge.

❹ The path soon becomes difficult as it travels through the gorge on private land. Climb the side of the gorge to reach the old railway line. The route follows the railway track back along the river.

❺ Eventually, the old track opens into clear fields. Cross the stile and follow the track under the bridge. Continue on the narrow track past a farm on the left. Head towards a corner of the field, keeping parallel to the river on the right. Pass the beehives to the left, cross the stile and turn immediately right towards the river. Continue on a narrow track downstream. At Old Bridge End Farm, cross the cattle grid and follow the farm road towards the A69.

❻ Cross the A69 to the lay-by at the start of the walk.

There has been a bridge over the River Tyne at Chollerford since Roman times – today's is a five-arched beauty.

access information

Travelling on the A69 from the west turn left on to the A6079 at the sign for Chollerford and then immediately right into a wide lay-by. From the east, pass the roundabout with the junction to Hexham and continue for another 300 m on the A69 before joining a sliproad to turn right on to the A6079 as above.

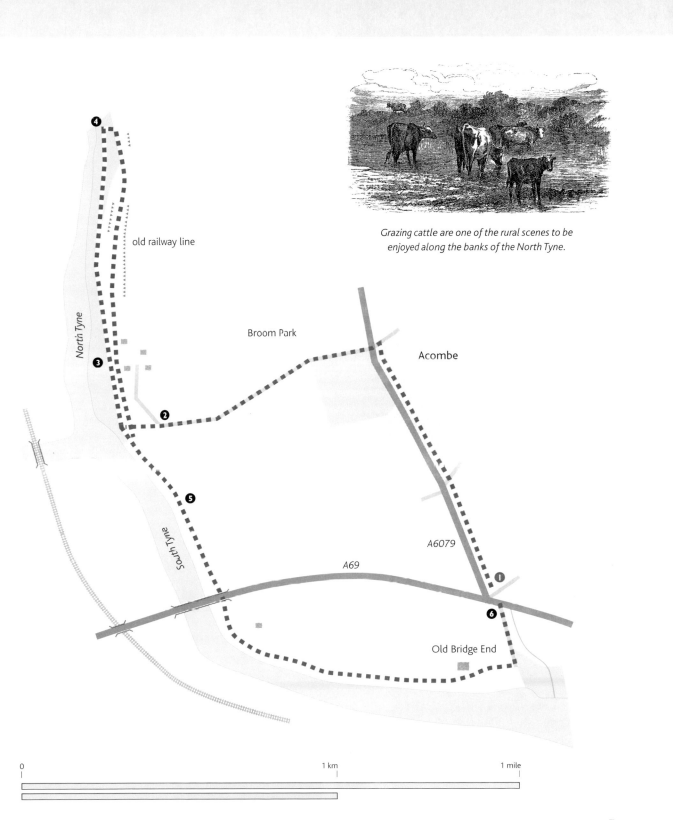

4

old railway line

North Tyne

3

Broom Park

Acombe

2

5

South Tyne

A6079

A69

I

6

Old Bridge End

Grazing cattle are one of the rural scenes to be enjoyed along the banks of the North Tyne.

| 0 | 1 km | 1 mile |

▲ Map: Explorer 316
▲ Distance: 10.6 km/6½ miles
▲ Walk ID: 724 Jude Howat

Difficulty rating

Time

▲ Sea, Pub, Toilets, Museum, Birds, Great Views

St Mary's Island from Tynemouth

This coastal walk begins at Tynemouth and heads through the popular resort of Whitley Bay to reach St Mary's Island where, tides permitting, you can visit the lighthouse via a causeway. The walk returns along the headland.

❶ From the car park, cross the road and head north along the promenade, past Cullercoats Bay. Keep to the pavement until you reach the clock.

❷ Take the steps to the lower level and head for the slipway down to the beach. Walk along the beach towards the lighthouse (St Mary's Island). At the far end of the bay, take the steps and then the path. Tides permitting, cross the causeway to visit the lighthouse. Return via the causeway.

❸ After crossing the causeway, continue straight ahead and follow the road for a short distance. There is a nature reserve to the right, just beyond the car park. As the road bends sharply to the right, leave it and take the path to the left. This path is not shown as a public footpath on the map but is well used.

❹ There are many paths coming in from the right along the coast – ignore all of these and continue straight ahead. When you reach the hump-backed bridge, cross over to continue for a short distance along the coastal footpath.

❺ Take the left-hand path, towards the sea again. This takes you down to the lower level of the promenade. After a short distance you will see a path heading back up the dunes. Take this path to continue past a small outdoor auditorium. Take the left-hand fork along the coast.

❻ Towards the end of the bay, the promenade paths come to an end. Rejoin the promenade alongside the road. Retrace your steps along the coast and back towards the start point.

further information

St Mary's Island has a lighthouse, which was built in 1898 and remained operational until 1984. The island is now run as a visitor centre, with the surrounding area maintained as a nature reserve. It is advisable to check the tide table for the area before commencing this walk.
Tel: 0191 200 8650,
http://www.ntb.org.uk/keepdate/tides.asp.

Ideally, this walk should be done at low tide so that you can cross the causeway to visit the lighthouse on St Mary's Island.

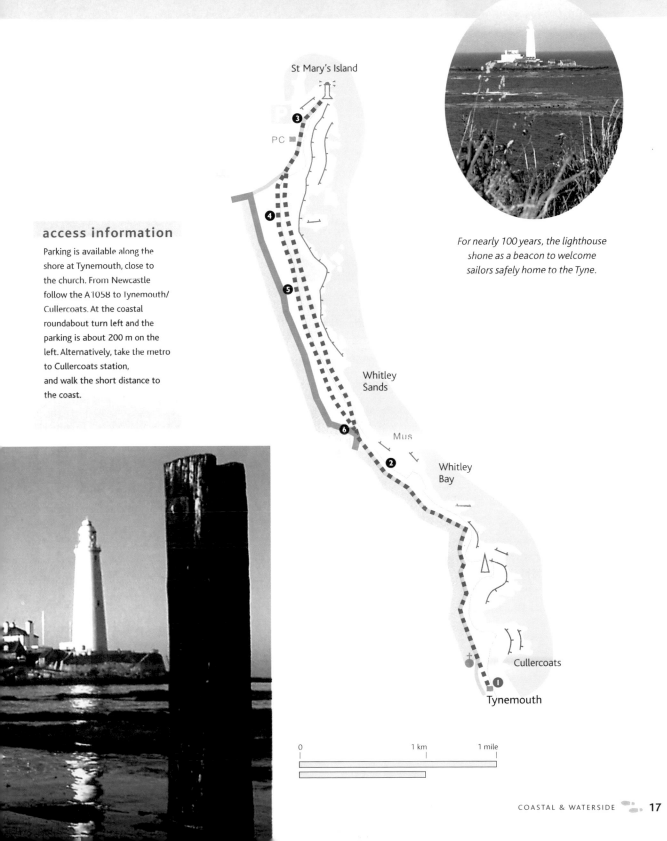

St Mary's Island

PC

❸

❹

❺

❻

❷

Whitley
Sands

Mus

Whitley
Bay

Cullercoats

❶

Tynemouth

access information

Parking is available along the
shore at Tynemouth, close to
the church. From Newcastle
follow the A1058 to Tynemouth/
Cullercoats. At the coastal
roundabout turn left and the
parking is about 200 m on the
left. Alternatively, take the metro
to Cullercoats station,
and walk the short distance to
the coast.

*For nearly 100 years, the lighthouse
shone as a beacon to welcome
sailors safely home to the Tyne.*

| 0 | | 1 km | | 1 mile |

Blanchland Circular Walk

From the picturesque village of Blanchland this walk takes you through the village square to reach the River Derwent. The narrow path then picks its way along the river to return to the village via a short section of road.

❶ Leaving the car park, turn right and walk into the square in the centre of the village. Pass under a stone arch and continue through the square to reach the bridge over the River Derwent. Do not cross the bridge.

❷ Just before the bridge, take the public footpath, then join the riverside path. Turn left at the riverbank and follow the path along the river.

❸ Cross the double stile and continue along the river bank, passing an old barn in the fields to the left. Just after the barn, fork left to join a farm track. Follow the track, first up the hill and then left, along the hillside.

❹ On reaching the road, keep straight ahead and continue along the hillside and down into the village again. At the old village church, turn right to return to the car park.

Even the bubbly, young River Derwent at Blanchland runs out of gurgle during a dry spell.

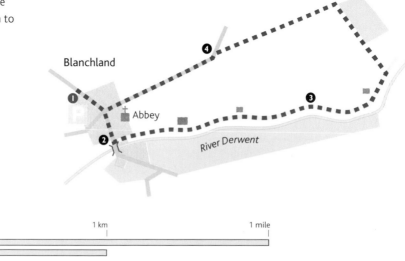

access information

Blanchland is off the A68, on the B6278 to Blanchland and Edmundbyers.

0   1 km   1 mile

▲ Map: Explorer OL 31
▲ Distance: 6 km/3¾ miles
▲ Walk ID: 320 Jude Howat

Difficulty rating

Time

▲ Hills, Wildlife, Lake, Waterfall, Nature Trail

Cauldron Snout from Cow Green Reservoir

This is the easy way to see the beautiful Cauldron Snout waterfalls. The walk follows the Teesdale National Nature Reserve nature trail, which is on a tarmac path along the side of the reservoir.

❶ Leave the car park and walk 300 m back along the road. At the marker turn right and follow the beginning of the nature trail. If you have a wheelchair with you, continue on the road for a further 400 m, then turn right. These routes will rejoin each other.

❷ When the narrow path reaches a T-junction with a wider path, turn left. Continue on this path, then take the tarmac path and go straight on. Pass through the stile, which is wide enough for a wheelchair. Follow the track along the side of the reservoir.

❸ Continue straight ahead, ignoring the junction to the right. Just before a small bridge over the river you will see a path off to the left. The path is a bit of a scramble and the rocks can be very slippery – this is the only part of the walk that is not suitable for wheelchairs. The path leads you to the waterfall.

❹ After enjoying views of Cauldron Snout, return by the same route to the car park.

further information

Come prepared for chilly, wet, windy weather as the hills are very exposed and even in summer it can be very cold. The route is good for wheelchairs, but the path to the waterfalls is not accessible.

access information

Follow the B6282 from Middleton-in-Teesdale past High Force. Turn left at Langdon Beck. Follow signs to Cow Green Reservoir.

Teesdale offers some of the most beautiful rolling countryside in England.

▲ Map: Explorer 308
▲ Distance: 8.86 km/5½ miles
▲ Walk ID: 400 Jude Howat

Difficulty rating

Time

▲ Sea, Pub, Toilets, Church, Birds,
Flowers, Food Shop, Good for Kids,
Industrial Archaeology, Mostly Flat,
Public Transport

Easington Colliery from Seaham Hall Beach

This linear walk leads you along Seaham Beach and headland, along the shore of Hawthorn Hive, to climb up to Easington Colliery. On the way you pass through two areas maintained by the National Trust.

1 Follow the yellow-chip path towards the sea. At the blue marker, turn right out of the car park. Follow the road to the next blue marker and climb the steps. Walk through another car park. Follow the road and the blue markers, crossing straight over the roundabout. Turn left into Foundry Road and pass the factory.

2 Turn right, following the cycle route on to Ropery Walk. Pass under both bridges, cross the road, then pass back under one of the bridges. Take the next footpath and follow it back to the road. Turn left at the next junction and continue.

3 At the roundabout follow the rough path on the left, heading towards the sea. This opens out into a track, which leads all the way to Nose's Point car park. Just before the hill, take the path leading off to the left. Follow this down a steep bank, to rise again at the far side. This leads you into a National Trust area.

4 Cross the bridge and turn left. Walk through the grasses towards Hawthorn Dene. At the yellow marker continue straight ahead. This is another National Trust area. Cross the railway line. Follow the steps down to the shore. Turn right and walk towards the cliffs (Hive Point). Turn right at the end of the bay and follow the path, crossing the stream under the viaduct. Continue up the hill.

5 At the T-junction of paths, turn left and follow the coastal footpath underneath the viaduct again and along the railway. Just before the railway bridge, keep left and walk towards the edge of the headland. Follow the path along the cliff, then back inland.

6 Continue towards Easington Colliery, following the path under the railway bridge. Go through the car park and walk to the corner of the main road. The bus stop is straight ahead.

Once a thriving coal mining community, there is no colliery at Easington any more – it was closed in 1993 and demolished in 1994.

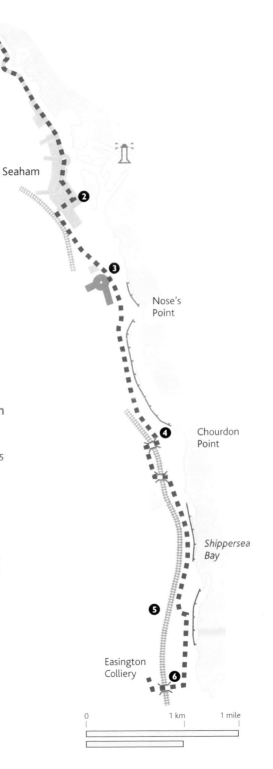

PC

❶

Seaham
Hall

Seaham

❷

❸

Nose's
Point

❹ Chourdon
Point

*Shippersea
Bay*

❺

Easington
Colliery **❻**

0   1 km   1 mile

*This impressive viaduct is a
monument to the area's
industrial history.*

access information

From the A19, leave at the
junction towards Seaham &
Dalton-le-Dale. Follow the B1285
northwards towards Sunderland,
which takes you through the
westernmost edge of Seaham.
Turn right at the traffic lights,
where the A19 is signposted to
the left, just beyond a school on
your right. Follow the lane down
towards the coast. There is good
parking here.

▲ Map: Explorer 305
▲ Distance: 7.5 km/4½ miles
▲ Walk ID: 325 Jude Howat

Difficulty rating

Time

River, Pub, Church, Wildlife, Birds, Flowers

Escomb from Bishop Auckland

The walk begins by the banks of the River Wear, close to the marketplace in Bishop Auckland, and takes you along the banks of the river towards the small village of Escomb, before descending back to Broken Bank, and back to the car park.

❶ From the car park, walk along the bank of the river, passing under the viaduct. Climb the steps to the road and turn left. After 20 m turn right on to the road and head towards the rugby club.

❷ As you approach the open grassy area take the path heading off to the right, which is on the river's edge. Follow this path round to a small car park. Follow the sign, which points uphill towards the trees. A yellow marker highlights the path, where it enters into the bushes.

❸ En route to Escomb take the path going downhill to the right. Continue over the stile and follow the path along the river. Cross the bridge, continuing along the river.

❹ At Escomb, walk up to the central square, where there is a Saxon church. Keep to the left side of the square. Take the next road to the left (Bede Close). Do not take the first public path, but continue further up the hill and follow the bridleway path, over the railway line.

❺ Pass through the gate and turn left. Follow the good path behind the houses until you reach the next road.

❻ At the road, turn left and follow the track down the hill and back over the railway. Once at this point, return using the same route as earlier to take you back to the car park.

County Durham offers the walker views of patchwork fields, dry-stone walls and grazing cattle.

access information

Bishop Auckland can be reached by either the A688 or the A689 west of the A1. Follow signs for the town centre then the marketplace. Take the small road to Binchester Fort. The car park is at the foot of the hill, by the river.

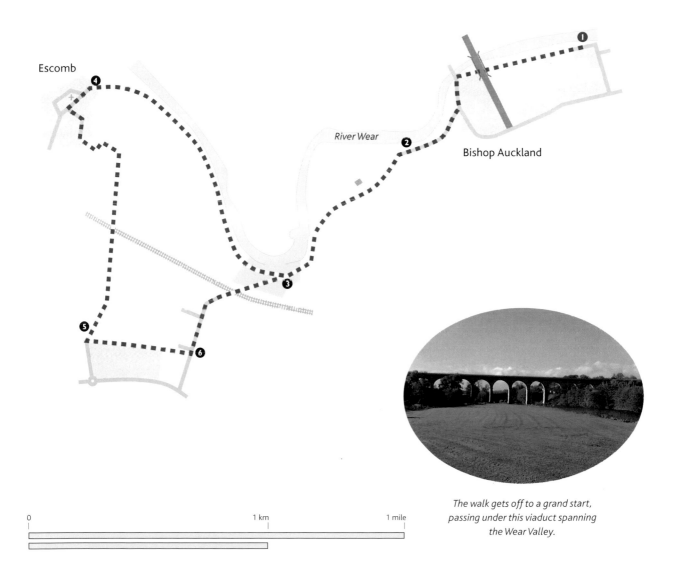

Escomb

River Wear

Bishop Auckland

0   1 km   1 mile

The walk gets off to a grand start, passing under this viaduct spanning the Wear Valley.

▲ Map: Explorer 305
▲ Distance: 10.47 km/6½ miles
▲ Walk ID: 1233 M. Parkin

Difficulty rating

Time

▲ Wildlife, Birds, River, Woodland

Whitworth Hall Country Park from Sunderland Bridge

The walk starts from the old Sunderland Bridge, passing through Coldstream Woods, over fields and lanes to Whitworth Hall Country Park, returning along the bank of the River Wear.

1 Start from the old Sunderland Bridge, opposite the entrance to the Croxdale Estate. Follow the track to pass under the Croxdale Viaduct and along the riverside to a bend in the river. Take the left fork into the trees and keep to the edge of the wood.

2 Bear right and cross a bridge over Nickynack Beck. Enter Coldstream Wood, looking out for roe deer. Leave the wood over a stile. Follow the path, crossing the track to Coldstream Farm. Continue over several stiles to reach a country lane. Turn left, then right, down to the end of a second lane. Outside the sewerage works' gates, head through the trees.

3 Leave the main path, and take the path on the right. Cross Valley Burn over a bridge. Climb up through the wood and follow the track skirting the housing estate. At the end of the estate continue along the farm track past the drive to Burton Beck Farm. Follow the track through a band of trees and over Burton Beck. Where the track bends right, head along an enclosed footpath on the left.

4 The footpath emerges on to a field. At a kissing gate follow the path as it passes to the other side of the fence. At the Whitworth Road turn right, passing the entrance to Whitworth Hall Country Park. Continue on the footpath to cross Page Bank Bridge.

5 Take the footpath to the right and follow the river. Cross the stile ahead. Continue along the riverside to cross another stile. Leave the river going diagonally left. Cross a small beck and pass through the kissing gate.

6 On the broad track turn right and pass under the Croxdale Viaduct. Walk along the track to the Sunderland Bridge, where the walk started.

access information

The old Sunderland Bridge spans the River Wear just off the A167 Durham to Croxdale road. Turn off the A167 near Croxdale Bridge and on to the B6300, then left down the lane, where there is ample parking before and after the bridge.

The handsome four-arched Sunderland Bridge over the River Wear is a good gathering point for the start of the walk.

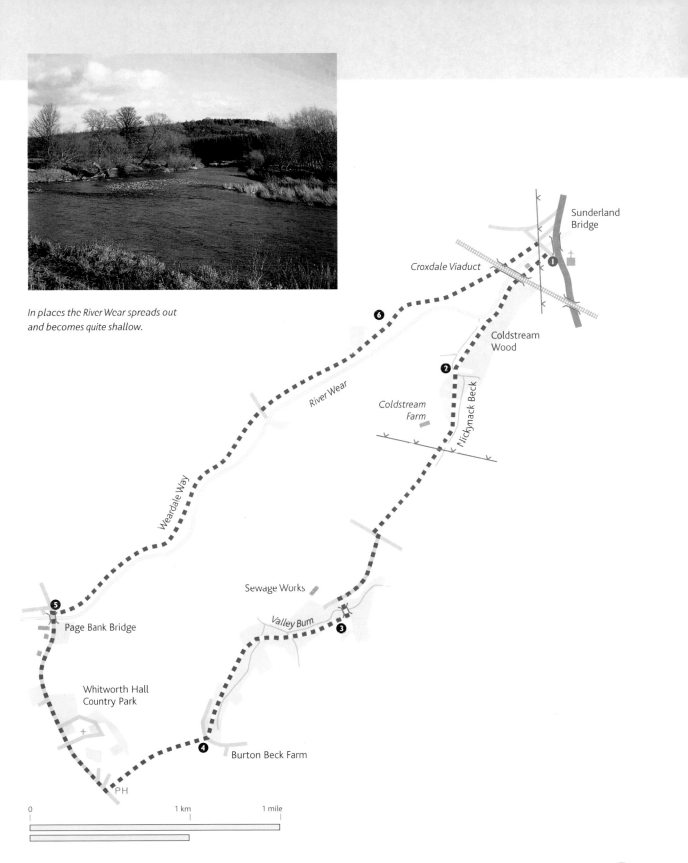

In places the River Wear spreads out and becomes quite shallow.

Sunderland Bridge

Croxdale Viaduct

Coldstream Wood

❶

❷

Nickynack Beck

Coldstream Farm

River Wear

❻

Weardale Way

Sewage Works

Valley Burn

❸

❺

Page Bank Bridge

Whitworth Hall Country Park

❹

Burton Beck Farm

PH

0   1 km   1 mile

▲ Map: Explorer OL 31
▲ Distance: 9.66 km/6 miles
▲ Walk ID: 33 Maggie Davey

Difficulty rating

Time

▲ River, Wildlife, Castle, Pub

Lartington Hall from Barnard Castle

This delightful walk follows the River Tees, a section of disused railway and some woodland to reach Lartington Hall. The Hall has fascinating medieval field systems, protected under the Countryside Stewardship Scheme.

❶ From Barnard Castle cross the bridge over the Tees and then take the B6277 towards Lartington. Just after the bridge, turn left on to the track alongside the stream. Cross the bridge over a small stream and bear left, back towards the river. Then take the path on the right.

❷ Follow the path up the hill. Join a track, which leads to the Deepdale Viaduct. Beyond the viaduct, turn right on to the path. Follow the disused railway line, passing the old signal box. Turn right on to the road and walk down through Lartington village.

❸ Take the left fork and continue to Lartington Hall. Walk down the drive, which leads to the back of the Hall. Keep on the road as it goes past a small outbuilding, and follow the sign to Barnard Castle. Go through the gate and follow the path along the stream. Turn left, cross the bridge and continue up the road.

❹ Just above the caravan site, turn right over the stile. Follow the path into the woods. The path emerges next to a cottage. Turn right on to the track, back towards Barnard Castle.

further information

Deepdale Viaduct was a magnificent steel structure which spanned the valley – it was taken down following the Beeching Report in 1963.

access information

Barnard Castle is a short distance along the A66 from Scotch Corner.

While in the area, take time to explore the ruins of Barnard Castle.

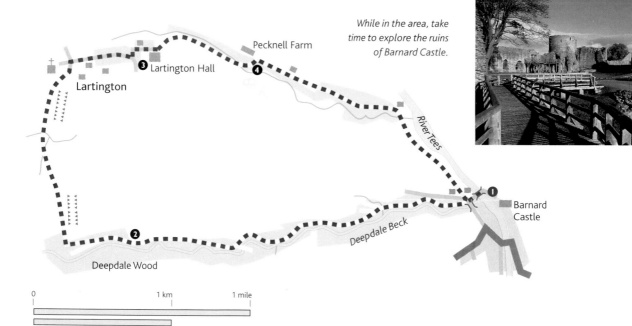

▲ Map: Explorer OL 21

▲ Distance: 5 km/3 miles

▲ Walk ID: 1104 Barry Smith

Difficulty rating

Time

Lake, Wildlife, Great Views,
Ancient Monument, Good for Kids

Oxygrains from Ripponden

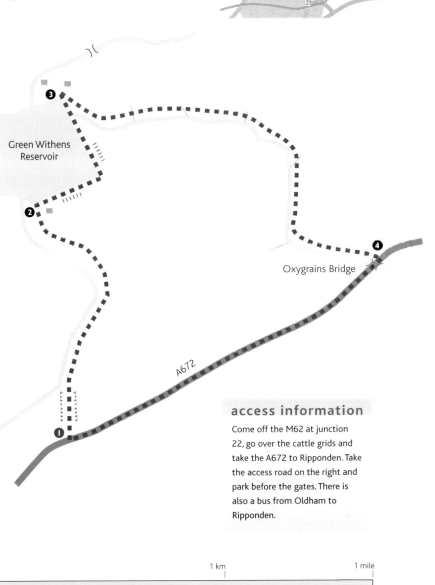

*Green Withens
Reservoir.*

This short walk takes in Green Withens Clough and Oxygrains,
with two bridges at the far end on the A672. A gentle climb
back up the road takes you back to your car.

1 Cross the road to the gates with
the sign for Green Withens Reservoir.
Go through a stone stile with a signpost,
leading to the top of the hill. Where the
tarmac road turns into a gravel track,
bear right. Continue to Green Withens
Reservoir Sailing Club.

2 At the sailing club car park, go right
through a large gate and continue on the
reservoir embankment. Bear left at the
corner, passing Green Withens Clough.

3 Just after passing a solar panel there
is a signposted path to the right,
directing the walk to Oxygrains Bridge.
Take the path next to the run-off
channel, not the one that the sheep
are on. Descend on the path and
down some steps.

4 After dropping down the valley,
through Green Withens Clough and
Oxygrains, you will emerge at the exit
on to the A672. Turn right and follow the
road back to the car.

further information

Oxygrains Bridge crosses a tributary
stream to the River Ryburn at
Rishworth. The stream flows down to
Booth Wood Reservoir via the much
smaller Spa Clough and Booth Dean
reservoirs. The name Oxygrains comes
from 'Osc', which is an old word for
water, and 'grains', referring to the
joining of two streams.

access information

Come off the M62 at junction
22, go over the cattle grids and
take the A672 to Ripponden. Take
the access road on the right and
park before the gates. There is
also a bus from Oldham to
Ripponden.

0   1 km   1 mile

▲ Map: Explorer OL 30
▲ Distance: 5.6 km/3¹/₂ miles
▲ Walk ID: 492 Jude Howat

Difficulty rating

Time

▲ Hills or Fells, River, Pub, Great Views

Reeth from Arkengarthdale

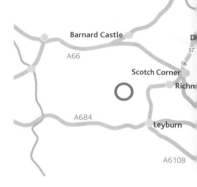

This is a charming, easy-to-follow short walk, with some great views to enjoy along the way. The route starts in the village of Reeth and goes along one side of Arkengarthdale, then returns on the opposite side.

❶ Starting by the village green with your back to the Black Bull pub, turn left and walk across the crossroads to follow the road out of the village.

❷ Just after a sharp left bend in the road, watch out for a waymarker by the trees. Follow the footpath across several small fields. You will need to cross lots of very narrow stiles between the fields, but the route is easy to follow, and each stile is marked with yellow paint. The path runs up the length of Arkengarthdale.

❸ Follow the path first round to the right, then over Arkle Beck. The path then climbs on the other side of the dale. After a short climb, turn right and head towards the nearest of the farmhouses, following the yellow markers through the garden and beyond.

❹ Continue on the path as it leads back towards Reeth on the opposite side of the dale. After a while the path drops to pass through a wood, close to the beck. Follow the bridleway slightly up the hill again. Continue to reach open countryside again, where there are good views of Reeth.

❺ Pass through a metal stile on your right, just after some trees, take a sharp right bend and cross the field to the right of a barn. Head towards the trees in the distance to reach another stile. Continue again towards the gate by the road.

❻ Pass through the gate, turn right and follow the road back up the hill to the village green.

access information

Take the A6108 west from Richmond. Reeth is on the B6270, which branches to the right before you reach Downholme. There is parking on the village green.

The glorious unspoilt beauty of Swaledale is the perfect antidote to the hurly burly of city life.

Arkengarthdale offers a beautiful
backdrop to much of the route
followed on this walk.

Arkengarthdale

Arkle Beck

Reeth

Mus

PH

0   1 km   1 mile

▲ Map: Explorer OL 21
▲ Distance: 8 km/5 miles
▲ Walk ID: 1130 W. Kembery

Difficulty rating

Time

▲ Hills or Fells, Lake/Loch, Birds, Great Views, Moor

The Gorple and Widdop Reservoirs from Hebden Bridge

From a remote spot above Hebden Bridge, the walk climbs steadily with views of both Lower and Upper Gorple reservoirs to reach Gorple Gate at the top of the moor. A steady descent takes in Widdop reservoir and continues for a gentle return along its shore.

❶ Turn right and walk down the quiet moorland road. Pass a house on the left and a road also on the left, to arrive opposite another lay-by. Turn right at the junction, following the route signposted 'Bridleway Lower Gorple'. Follow the track to a junction at the start of the reservoir.

❷ Turn right, following the signpost marked 'Permissive Footpath Upper Gorple', still on a track.

❸ Do not cross the dam. Turn right on a narrow path, signposted Widdop.

❹ At the top (Gorple Gate), turn right at the sign marked 'Public Bridleway Widdop Road' and follow the broad track downhill. As the track swings sharply right, go straight ahead on a narrow footpath, indicated by a marker. The path follows a broken wall above the reservoir on the right.

❺ At a fingerpost, turn right to cross a wooden bridge and walk up to join a broad green footpath. Turn right at the sign for Widdop Dam and continue with the reservoir on the right.

❻ At the metal bridge keep to the right of the wall (this path is not marked on the map). Almost immediately you will arrive at a wooden bridge and a junction of footpaths. Turn right to cross the bridge and then turn left to follow a path to the left of the reservoir alongside the deep drain. After passing two houses, bear left to cross a bridge and go up to the road via a gate. Turn right along the road to return to the car park.

further information

There is no public transport nearby. Park at the southern end of Widdop Reservoir by the dam on a large concreted area.

access information

The walk starts from a very remote location on the quiet, narrow unclassified road between Nelson and Hebden Bridge.

As well as being surrounded by lovely Yorkshire countryside, Hebden Bridge is fast becoming a lively cultural and social centre.

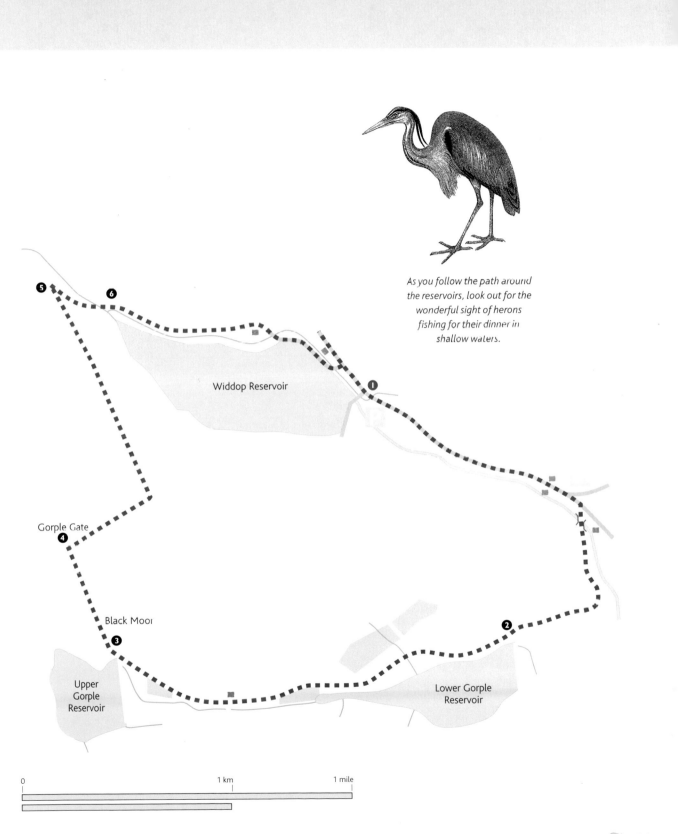

As you follow the path around the reservoirs, look out for the wonderful sight of herons fishing for their dinner in shallow waters.

Widdop Reservoir

Gorple Gate

Black Moor

Upper Gorple Reservoir

Lower Gorple Reservoir

0   1 km   1 mile

▲ Map: Explorer OL 2
▲ Distance: 11 km/7 miles
▲ Walk ID: 113 L. and D. Fishlock

Difficulty rating

Time

▲ Hills or Fells, River, Pub, Toilets,
Wildlife, Birds, Flowers, Great Views

Linton and Burnsall from Grassington

This undemanding walk takes you through the delightful little villages of Burnsall and Linton, ending with a visit to the beautiful Linton waterfall to complete a truly enjoyable family day out.

❶ Go through the gate at the back of the car park. Turn right, following the sign to Linton Falls. At the junction before Linton Falls, turn left on to the riverside path. Follow the footpath sign away from the river to a stile on to the lane. Turn right.

❷ At the junction, follow the signed footpath to Burnsall. Cross a field, a footbridge and a kissing gate, to follow the river again. Turn right to cross the Hebden suspension bridge and then left towards Burnsall. Cross a stone stile to continue along the riverbank.

❸ Turn right before Burnsall Bridge. When the road turns right, take the left path, crossing a number of fields, lanes and stiles. Continue in the same direction, following the footpath signs and crossing Startan Beck. Go through the stile and straight on. Pass through a gate and exit the field through a stile in the corner. Turn left along the lane through Thorpe.

❹ Take the left fork. Continue along the lane, then cross a gated stile on your right. Follow the path through the field. Just after the footpath sign, continue ahead and cross the next stile and field. Go through the farmyard, then turn right along the road to enter Linton.

❺ At the T-Junction, turn left across the bridge and take the footpath on the right, along Linton Beck (signpost to

Threshfield). Follow the path to the right, in front of Linton Country Crafts and then between dry stone walls. Take the right fork, continuing under the old railway bridge. Cross the field, over a small stream towards a small strip of woodland. Cross the main road. Take the path on your left to Threshfield School and turn right.

❻ Turn left along Church Road. Take the path on the left to Linton Falls. Turn right just before a small bridge and cross Linton Falls Bridge. Retrace the route to the car park.

access information

The walk starts from the National Park Information Centre just off the B6265 Grassington-Hebden road (fee payable). Bus services to the park operate from Leeds, Bradford and York.

Grassington is a charming village of traditional stone cottages and cobbled streets in Upper Wharfedale at the heart of the Yorkshire Dales National Park.

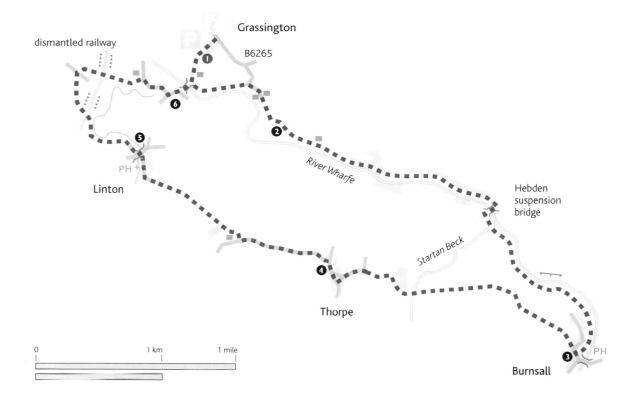

dismantled railway

Grassington

B6265

River Wharfe

Hebden suspension bridge

Startan Beck

Linton

PH

Thorpe

Burnsall

PH

0   1 km   1 mile

▲ Map: Explorer OL 30
▲ Distance: 8.25 km/5 miles
▲ Walk ID: 1057 Steve Murray

Difficulty rating

Time

▲ Hills or Fells, River, Pub, Wildlife,
Great Views, Waterfall, Woodland

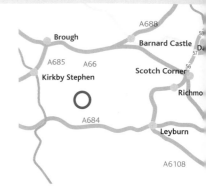

Keld from Muker

A dales walk with some magnificent views and waterfalls, commencing in Muker, and taking you up the east side of the dale to reach Keld. The walk returns to Muker via a section of the Pennine Way along North Gang Scar.

1 Park in the lay-by opposite the school. Turn right, walking towards Muker. At the first junction, turn left and follow the road uphill through the village. Continue to the top of the hill, branch right and aim towards the right of the far terrace. Pass through the stile and follow the path along the slabs, across the fields towards the river.

2 Turn right and cross the river, via the footbridge. Follow the path up the bank to reach another fingerpost. At the top of the steps turn left and follow the bridleway along the side of the dale. The path steadily rises, before dropping down to a footbridge by a waterfall at Swinner Gill. The path then climbs steeply, providing spectacular views.

3 Continue past a cottage as the path turns sharply to the left, then begins to drop towards Keld. Follow the path down to another waterfall and cross a footbridge. At the next junction, turn left down by the trees and cross a footbridge over the River Swale. Bear right through a gate and walk up a steep path.

4 Turn left at the top, to follow the Pennine Way signs. The path continues to climb, with views of the river below. At the fingerpost go straight ahead, beneath a steep cliff on your right. At the next fingerpost, bear right.

5 Follow the grassy track along the edge of North Gang Scar to reach a T-junction of paths.

6 Bear left along a walled track and follow it down into Muker and back to your start point.

At Keld, you have the chance of taking a nostalgic trip on an old steam train, on the North Yorkshire Moors Railway.

access information

From the A1 follow the sign to Richmond. Passing Richmond take the A6108 until you reach the junction with the B6270. Take this junction and follow the road as it takes you through Swaledale. Pass through Muker and park in the lay-by opposite the school.

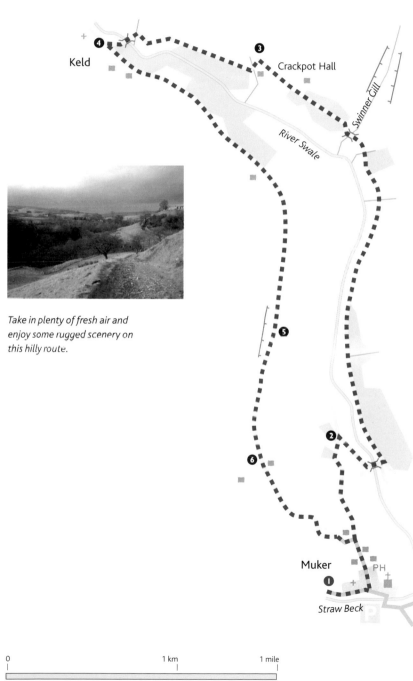

Keld

4

3 Crackpot Hall

Swinner Gill

River Swale

Take in plenty of fresh air and
enjoy some rugged scenery on
this hilly route.

This walk through the Yorkshire
Dales will take you along winding
tracks, past dry-stone walls
and buildings.

5

2

6

Muker

PH

1

Straw Beck

0   1 km   1 mile

▲ Map: Explorer OL 43
▲ Distance: 12.08 km/7½ miles
▲ Walk ID: 300 Jude Howat

Difficulty rating

!!!

Time

●●●●

▲ Hills or Fells, Lake/Loch, Pub, Toilets, Museum, National Trust/NTS, Wildlife, Birds, Flowers, Great Views, Food Shop

Peel Crags from Housesteads

This hilly walk takes in an impressive section of Hadrian's Wall, from Housesteads to the end of Peel Crags. There are some spectacular views before the walk returns along more gentle slopes.

1 Follow the path through the arch and up the hill towards the Housesteads Fort. When you reach the museum continue up the hill on the outside of the fort, towards the trees on the brow of the hill. Pass through the gate and walk along the top of the wall. Stay on the path that follows the wall's route.

2 Cross the stile on to the farmer's road, then turn right and cross a second stile. Continue along the route of the wall on the northern side.

3 Descend from the wall and cross the field towards the house. Cross the stile and continue down the hill by turning left on the road. Cross the B6318 and continue past the Once Brewed Visitor Centre.

4 Take the first junction on the left, towards Vindolanda. When you reach the Vindolanda car park, continue down the track on the outside of the wall. At the signpost, ignore its arrow and stick to the road up the hill. Turn left when you reach the T-junction, then follow the road.

5 At the next junction turn right and continue until you reach a bridleway on the left. Take this bridleway up to East Crindledykes Farm and continue over the field beyond. Beware – the field sometimes contains a bull!

6 Cross the stile, then turn right and follow the road back to the car park at Housesteads.

access information

Housesteads is on the B6318, which runs parallel to the A69 west of Newcastle. There is pay and display parking at the visitor centre for Housesteads.

A visit to Hadrian's Wall is a must for anyone living in or visiting the north of England.

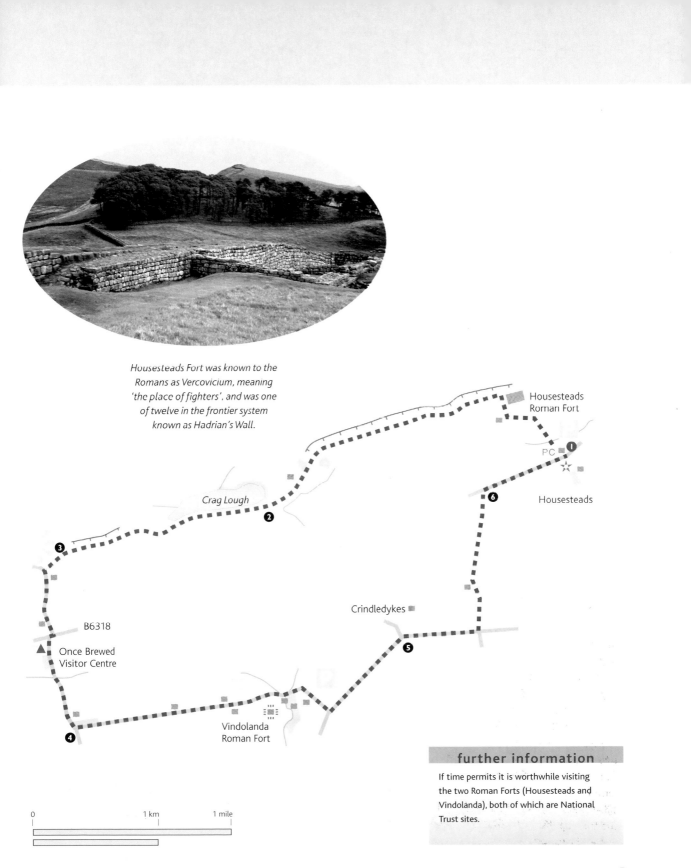

Housesteads Fort was known to the
Romans as Vercovicium, meaning
'the place of fighters', and was one
of twelve in the frontier system
known as Hadrian's Wall.

Housesteads
Roman Fort

PC

Housesteads

Crag Lough

B6318

Once Brewed
Visitor Centre

Crindledykes

Vindolanda
Roman Fort

0   1 km   1 mile

▲ Map: Explorer OL 42
▲ Distance: 9.6 km/6 miles
▲ Walk ID: 427 Jude Howat

Difficulty rating

Time

▲ Hills or Fells, Great Views

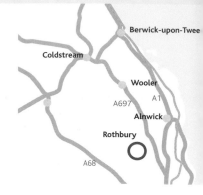

Simonside Crags from Lordenshaws

This is a wonderfully bracing ridge walk, which takes in the four peaks of **The Beacon Cairn, Dove Crag, Simonside Crags and Lordenshaws Fort,** with breathtaking views along the way.

❶ Follow the rocky footpath up the hill, and take the first right fork to continue towards The Beacon Cairn. The path follows a high-level ridge and offers superb views. Cross over the stile and continue uphill towards the summit of Dove Crag.

❷ Just before you reach the summit, take the left fork and follow the broad track which leads to a cairn. Continue along the ridge-top path. The path passes to the right of Old Stell Crag, leading to the summit directly above Simonside Crags. At the summit, descend via a steep path down the face of the crag to join a forest track.

❸ Turn right on to the track. It bends left sharply, then descends into the forest. At the marker, turn right. Pass by a bridge on the right and continue down the hill to reach a grassy picnic area.

❹ Aim diagonally right across the grass to join a short path, which leads to the road. Turn left on to the bridleway, just beyond the cattle grid, and head up a small hill. Past the quarry the path turns to the right, through a gate. Continue along the path, and through a further two gates, to reach Whitton Hillhead Farm. At the farm, turn right on to the farm track.

❺ At the next junction turn right. Follow the track up the hill to Whittondean and Lordenshaws Fort.

❻ Near the top of the hill, take the left path to go up to the fort (then retrace your steps to this point). Continue straight ahead to reach the car park.

The views around Rothbury include stunning panoramas of peaks, crags and rolling countryside.

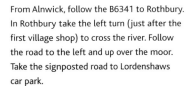

access information

From Alnwick, follow the B6341 to Rothbury.
In Rothbury take the left turn (just after the
first village shop) to cross the river. Follow
the road to the left and up over the moor.
Take the signposted road to Lordenshaws
car park.

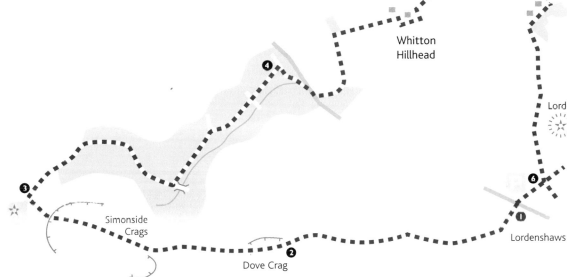

Whittondean

Whitton
Hillhead

Lordenshaws Fort

Simonside
Crags

Dove Crag

Lordenshaws

0   1 km   1 mile

*Lordenshaws is an Iron Age hill fort
surrounded by strange 'cup and ring'
stone carvings. This site alone makes
this walk one to savour.*

▲ Map: Explorer 340
▲ Distance: 16.1 km/10 miles
▲ Walk ID: 362 Dave Lingard

Difficulty rating

Time

▲ Hills or Fells, Lake/Loch, Church, Great Views

Carey Burn from North Middleton

From North Middleton the track climbs steadily up and over moorland. The walk descends to the Coldgate Burn then climbs up to an old farmstead. The return is downhill or flat and takes in the magnificent Carey Burn.

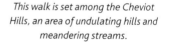

This walk is set among the Cheviot Hills, an area of undulating hills and meandering streams.

1 Head up the farm track to the top of the hill. Go through the gate and follow the path down over the burn. Cross the bridge. Follow the track across the field and over the stile.

2 Take the right-hand track uphill. Go over the stile and turn right. Head downhill, over a bridge, and follow the path, taking the footbridge across Harthope Burn. Go over the stile and turn right.

3 Cross the road and turn left, through the gate. Continue uphill on a farm track. Go over the stile and follow the grassy track, eventually heading downhill. Turn left on to the red-chipped farm track. At the waymarker, turn right. Cross the burn and climb the bank, heading for Broadstruther.

4 At Broadstruther follow the path to a marker, which directs you towards the red farm track in the valley. Avoid dropping down to the footbridge. Veer slightly left, above the burn, and head for the gate across another burn. Follow the path into Carey Burn, crossing over to the left bank. Keep to the right of the woods and follow Carey Burn as it bends.

5 Climb up above the burn to just below the scree slope, and follow the track, just short of the bridge. Cross the stile and turn left on to the road. Go over the stile, then follow the track across an open area. When the track suddenly turns right, go straight ahead over the stile. Cross the field to the gate on the far side, which leads you through a wood.

6 Cross the Coldgate Water by the footbridge. When you reach the road, turn right along it for a short walk back to the start point.

access information

North Middleton is 4 km south of Wooler, Northumberland. The unclassified road on which the hamlet stands runs parallel to the A697 trunk road and can be accessed at Wooler. Parking is available on the verge just south of the hamlet and close to the starting point.

The stunning slopes of the Cheviot Hills, on the border between England and Scotland, are famous as sheep-grazing land.

5

Carey Burn

4
Broadstruther

Harthope Burn

3

2

6   Coldgate
      Mill

Happy Valley

North
Middleton

1

0   1 km   1 mile

▲ Map: Explorer OL 43
▲ Distance: 4.8 km/3 miles
▲ Walk ID: 686 Jude Howat

Difficulty rating

Time

▲ Hills or Fells, Pub, Toilets, Castle, Great Views

Thirlwall Castle from Walltown

This short circular walk takes in part of Hadrian's Wall (between Walltown Quarry and Thirlwall Castle) and part of the Pennine Way. The walk provides lovely views, with relatively little effort!

1 Leave the car park and walk along the road to the T-junction. Turn right and continue for about 200 m, looking for a stile on the left.

2 Cross the stile and follow the wall along the hillside to join a farm track, heading steeply down the hill to the Tipalt Burn.

3 Cross the burn via the footbridge and follow the track up the hill on the far side, passing Thirlwall Castle on the way. Continue through the farmyard. Shortly after the farmyard, take the left fork and follow the path to Wood House.

4 At the junction, branch to the right and follow the road downhill towards the burn again. Cross the burn via the stepping stones, then follow the sunken track to the left and uphill.

5 Turn right at the marker and head through the field towards the Low Old Shields farmhouse. Exit the field in its far left-hand corner, then pass between the

shed and main farm building. Continue through the farmyard to join the farm track at the front of the farmhouse. Follow the track uphill as it joins on to a rough road. Turn right as it becomes a proper road again, and follow the route back down towards (2).

6 This time, turn left on to the path at the end of the quarry picnic site. Follow the path, which runs parallel to the road taken at the beginning of the walk. The path leads back towards the car park.

This gentle walk takes in sights ranging from Hadrian's Wall to Tipalt Burn.

access information

From the A69 Haltwhistle to Brampton road, take the B6318 to Greenhead. In Greenhead, turn right up a steep hill for a short distance, then take the first road on the left (signposted to Walltown Quarry). Follow the quarry signs (turning right after a short distance) to the car park.

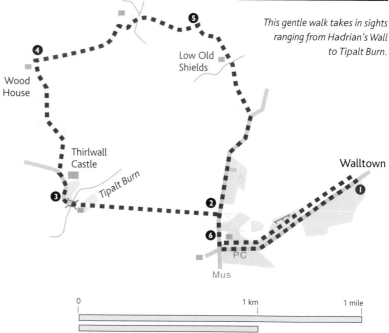

▲ Map: Explorer 305
▲ Distance: 12.88 km/8 miles
▲ Walk ID: 498 Karen Land

Difficulty rating

Time

▲ River, Great Views

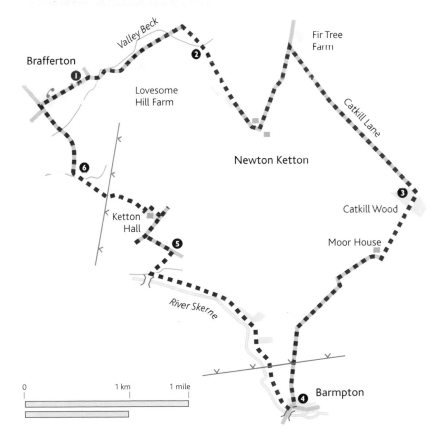

The kissing gate in front of Barmpton Hall.

Brafferton to Ketton Country

The village of Brafferton lies in a small area of rolling countryside steeped in history, known locally as 'Ketton Country'. The walk is an easy ramble along old tracks, green lanes and ancient highways of outstanding beauty.

❶ Walk up the main street. At the end, follow High House Lane across Valley Beck. Just before it bends left towards High House Farm, go through a field gate on the right. Walk ahead through the field along a tall hedge. Continue on to reach a signed farm gate and stile.

❷ Climb gently between the hedges. The lane descends through several gates to arrive at Newton Ketton. Turn left at the junction. Just before reaching Fir Tree Farm, turn right into the ancient Catkill Lane and continue for 2 km.

❸ Soon after the entrance into Catkill Wood, take the footpath on the right, to cut through dense scrub. Proceed straight on, through the fields. At Moor House, head to the left of the buildings and follow the farm track to Barmpton.

❹ Pass through a kissing gate in front of Barmpton Hall. Walk along the River Skerne until you reach the farm bridge, then bear right to reach the old Ketton packhorse bridge. Behind the bridge take the right fork.

❺ Turn left at the access road. At the top of the hill, turn right to pass Ketton Hall. Just beyond a small wood, locate a green farm gate on the left. Follow the wood away. When it ends, continue straight on and through the bridle gate. Follow the left boundary fence to go through another gate. Veer right and stay near the hedge over the next two fields.

❻ At the far corner of the last field a pair of gates leads on to a quiet green lane that heads back to Brafferton.

access information

Brafferton is on an unclassified road off the A167 north of Darlington. Roadside parking is available in the village. There is also a regular bus service.

▲ Map: Explorer 308
▲ Distance: 6.44 km/4 miles
▲ Walk ID: 1063 Norman Hope

Difficulty rating

Time

▲ Pub, Stately Home, Birds, Butterflies, Woodland

Beamish Woods from Causey Arch

This is a picturesque walk over Causey Arch and around the woods of Beamish, taking in some of the industrial sights as well as the natural beauty of the surrounding area.

❶ Park the car at Causey Arch picnic site. (The picnic area contains not only the famous arch, but also a magnificent embankment and culvert built in 1725.) Take the path to the left of the toilets at the bottom of the car park. Follow the path down, keeping the embankment on your left. Cross the Causey Arch and follow the main path. On reaching a footbridge on the left, cross it and follow the path to the railway.

❷ Go through the kissing gate and cross the railway line, passing through the gate on the other side. Cross the open field and turn right at the main road. About 200 m down the road on the other side, the footpath continues up a flight of steps.

❸ Go over the stile and keep going until the path meets a narrow country lane. Turn left. On the road, about 50 m on the left, go through the doorway in the wall. Walk through Carricks Hill Wood, keeping to the main path. When you reach the T-junction, turn left. This path joins a main road. Turn right and walk towards Beamish Hall.

❹ About 200 m up the road, opposite Beamish Hall, follow the sign marked Coppy Lane.

❺ The lane joins Beamishburn Road near The Causey Arch Inn, where you turn left. After about 50 m turn right to cross the fields by the public footpath.

❻ The next road is the A6076. Cross it and go under the railway to return back to the start of the walk.

further information

From the Norman Conquest the lords of Beamish were also the lords of Tanfield and Kibblesworth. The first records of a grand house on the estate were in 1309 when Bertram Monboucher took a wife who brought the Beamish estate as her dowry. The National Coal Board moved its offices here in 1954 but gave up the hall and grounds in 1974 to Beamish Hall College, which now shares the premises with the North of England Open Air Museum.

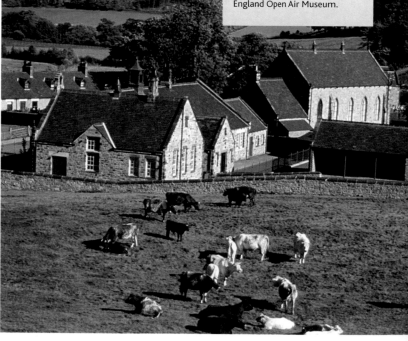

One of the most fascinating venues in this area is the Beamish North of England Open Air Museum.

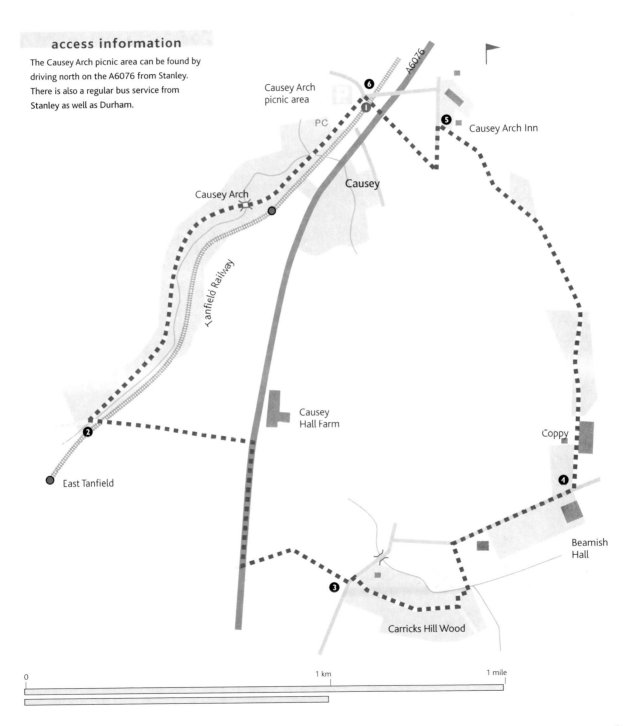

access information

The Causey Arch picnic area can be found by
driving north on the A6076 from Stanley.
There is also a regular bus service from
Stanley as well as Durham.

Causey Arch
picnic area

PC

A6076

❻

❶

❺ Causey Arch Inn

Causey Arch

Causey

Tanfield Railway

Causey
Hall Farm

❷

East Tanfield

Coppy

❶

Beamish
Hall

❸

Carricks Hill Wood

0

1 km

1 mile

▲ Map: Explorer OL 31
▲ Distance: 3 km/2 miles
▲ Walk ID: 808 Jude Howat

Difficulty rating

👣👣

Time

⬤

▲ River, Toilets, Play Area, Wildlife, Birds, Flowers, Great Views, Food Shop, Good for Kids, Tea Shop, Woodland

Hamsterley Forest from Bedburn

This short but enjoyable walk in Hamsterley Forest is ideal for when you need a breath of fresh air but time is limited. It takes you along both sides of the Bedburn Valley, through the forest, to return via the river.

❶ Exit the car park via the small path leading into the forest. At the immediate T-junction turn right towards the children's play area, following the yellow markers. Turn left at the next T-junction to join the larger track. Cross over the burn (via a bridge) and follow the track uphill, into the forest. At the T-junction, turn right to follow the track along the hillside, until you reach a forest road.

❷ Turn right, and descend for a short distance. Leave the road for the small path into the woods (signposted with a yellow marker). The path now begins to descend towards the river.

❸ Do not cross the first bridge over the river. Instead, keep to the right and follow the path along the riverbank. The path does not follow the river, but meanders close by. Cross at the next bridge and turn right to follow the riverside path.

❹ The adventure play area marks the end of the walk (the car park is just on its far side).

Both wild and arranged flowers add colour to the route as it heads off from Bedburn.

access information

Hamsterley Forest is close to the A68 near Bishop Auckland/Crook. There are brown tourist information signs from the junction close to Witton-le-Wear. Follow the signs, which lead into Hamsterley village. Keep following the signs through the village then out towards Bedburn. Park in the second car park.

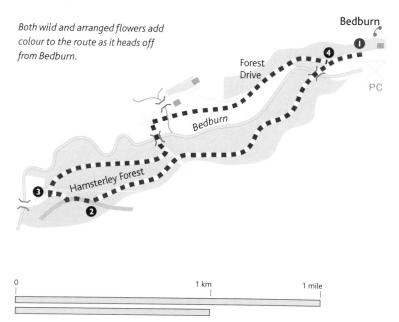

▲ Map: Explorer 304
▲ Distance: 9.66 km/6 miles
▲ Walk ID: 1034 M. Parkin

Difficulty rating

Time

▲ Wildlife, Birds, Great Views, Woodland

Whitcliffe Scar from Richmond

This tranquil walk passes through woods and fields above the River Swale, before returning along the heights of Whitcliffe Scar with enchanting views over Applegarth, Swaledale, and Richmond.

1 Follow the track to High Leases and through Whitcliffe Wood. Stay on the track as it passes below Whitcliffe Scar, heading towards East Applegarth Farm. Continue straight ahead on a green track, passing through a gateway and a field. Cross the road and follow the path on the left. Cross the next road and the stile ahead. Cross another two fields and a small stream.

2 Head left to pass West Applegarth Farm. Follow the farm road, until it reaches the old Richmond to Reeth road. Turn right on Clapgate Bank and pass a junction for Whashton and Ravensworth. Cross the cattle grid on the right.

3 Almost immediately, leave the farm road, taking the green path to the left towards the top of Whitcliffe Scar. You will pass two monuments on the way. Carry on along the top of the scar. Keep to the breast of the hill, for marvellous views of the Hambleton and Cleveland Hills, and Richmond Castle.

4 Go down the hill to reach High Leases. Turn left along the track, back to the start of the walk.

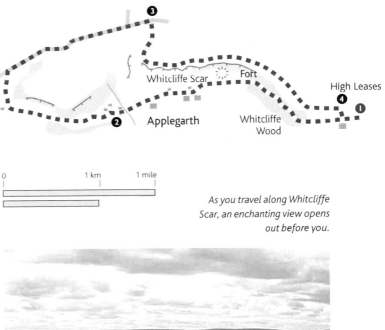

As you travel along Whitcliffe Scar, an enchanting view opens out before you.

access information

Heading out of Richmond on the main A6108 Reeth road, but before leaving the town at a sharp left, leave the main road and go up the avenue of West Fields. Follow the lane for just over a mile until the tarmac ends and park at the roadside between Whitcliffe and High Leases farms.

▲ Map: Explorer OL 27
▲ Distance: 4.03 km/2½ miles
▲ Walk ID: 843 Jude Howat

Difficulty rating

Time

▲ Hills or Fells, Birds, Flowers, Great
Views, Good for Kids, Woodland

Killing Nab Scar from Newtondale Holt

This walk follows a forestry commission track along the lower slopes of the scar, with a steep climb to reach Needle Point for spectacular views. After a steep descent, the walk follows the track at the foot of the hill, to return to the station.

❶ Head out of the station and follow the path to the Forestry Commission information board. Continue up the hill to join the main track.

❷ Turn right (following the green arrows) along the foot of the hills. Pass the first junction and continue following the track to the right.

❸ At the sign pointing into the trees, leave the main track and take the small path up the steps. At the end of the steps, the path becomes indistinct. Head up through the trees to reach another marker, then continue straight ahead. The path bends sharply back on itself to reach the top of the scar, where there are fantastic views.

❹ Follow the green marker, turning to the right. Stay on this high-level path to reach a main forest track. Follow the track sharply left, back into the trees. Continue to reach another section of forest track. Turn left at the forest track and walk about 20 m until you see another green arrow leading back off the main track. Follow the direction of the arrow back into the trees.

❺ As the descent begins, take the sharp left-hand junction in the path. The path now becomes much steeper and can be very wet underfoot. Carefully follow the path down the hillside to join the main forest track that you were on at the beginning of the walk. Turn left on to the main track and follow it back to (2).

❻ Turn right and then retrace your steps to the halt.

further information

Contact the North Yorkshire Moors Railway for further details of train times and costs: http://www.northyorkshiremoors railway.com/ or telephone: 01751 472508

This is the ideal walk for train enthusiasts! The only way to reach the start is by steam train on the North Yorkshire Moors Railway.

access information

Access to Newtondale Halt is only by means of the North Yorkshire Moors Railway (trains leave hourly from Grosmont and Pickering).

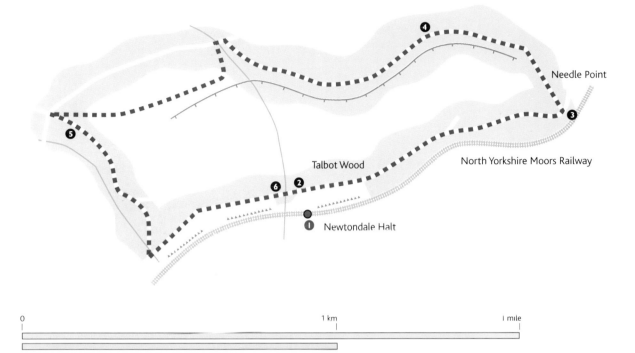

Needle Point

North Yorkshire Moors Railway

Talbot Wood

Newtondale Halt

0   1 km   1 mile

*Allow yourself time on
the walk to enjoy the
spectacular views from
Killing Nab Scar.*

Difficulty rating

Time

● ● ●

▲ Pub, Toilets, Museum, Play
Area, Church, Castle, Wildlife, Birds,
Flowers, Butterflies, Food Shop

Low Kettle Spring from Ripley

This is a circular walk along the Nidderdale Way, through stunning Yorkshire woodlands and farmland. The route also passes through the formal estate of Ripley Castle.

❶ From the car park head north through the village on the main road. Follow signs for the Nidderdale Way along Birthwaite Lane until reaching the B6165. Cross the road and follow the Nidderdale Way.

❷ Turn right into the wood and follow the path down the hill. At the marker at the bottom of the wood turn right. Follow the path through the fields, looking out for the ancient inscribed stone.

❸ Navigate the boggy ground and head left along the Nidderdale Way, passing along the edge of the wood. At the road, turn left and walk down the hill. Take the bridleway marked off to the right and follow it to the farm at the end of the track.

❹ Just before the farm, the footpath crosses the field to the left. Drop down the field to the stream. At the stream, turn right and follow it round a bend. Cross the stream at the bridge and head to the right, into the field.

❺ Follow the marker indicating the path across and up into the next field. Follow the path until meeting the road, and turn left. Go straight across the crossroads at Bedlam. The path goes through the garden gate alongside the main house gates. Walk through to a signed path across fields. Where the footpaths meet, head straight on

towards the stone estate wall at the top of the rise. At the wall, turn right and follow it round. Where the track meets a farm track, turn left.

❻ At the next junction turn left and follow the track back into Ripley. The car park is to the right, back along the main road.

access information

Ripley is on the A61 north of Harrogate. Car parking in free car park. Buses from Knaresborough.

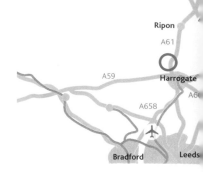

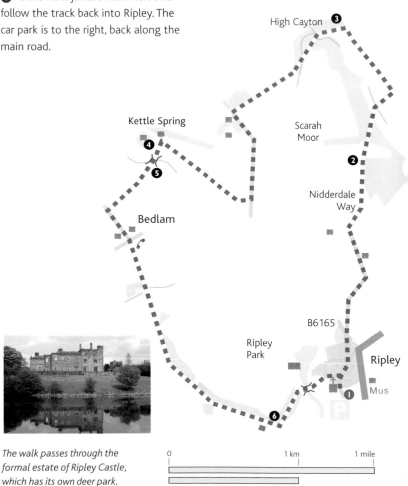

The walk passes through the formal estate of Ripley Castle, which has its own deer park.

0   1 km   1 mile

Difficulty rating

Time

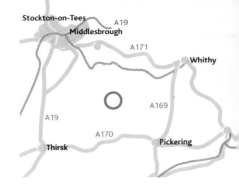

Low Mill from Church Houses

This pleasant stroll in Farndale (famous for its daffodils) in the North York Moors starts in Church Houses, passing through Low Mill to return over fields and through farmyards.

❶ The walk starts from the lane behind the pub in Church Houses. Go through the gate and follow the lane to High Mill (The Daffy Caffy). Pass through the yard and exit through the gate. Follow the path near the River Dove's banks.

❷ At the junction, go through the gate and continue straight on, with the river on your right.

❸ Cross the footbridge. Follow the path up to reach a country lane in the delightful hamlet of Low Mill and stop for a visit. Retrace your steps to cross back over the footbridge. Go straight ahead and cross the field to the hedge. Keeping the hedge on your right, continue to High Wold House farm.

❹ Go through the gate and cross the yard, exiting on to a track on the left. Pass through a gate just below Cote Hill Farm. Cross the field diagonally left and climb over the stile. Pass the cottage on the right and cross the field to reach Bitchagreen Farm. Go through the gate and cross the yard to exit over the stile. Cross the field to climb another stile on to a track leading to Bragg Farm ahead.

❺ Go straight through the farmyard and exit through the gate. Cross the field and continue into the next one. Keep the wall to the left and cross the stile in the facing wall. Turn immediately right along the wall to reach a gate on to the road. Turn left and continue to Church Houses.

❻ At the crossroads outside the pub in Church Houses, turn left and down the lane to the start of the walk.

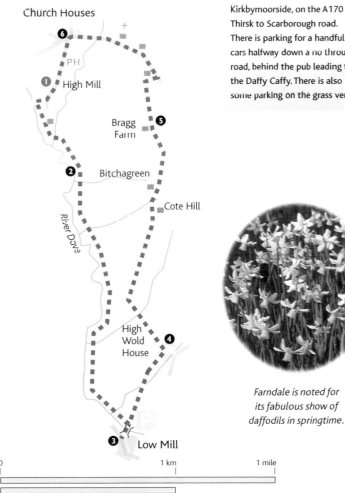

access information

Church Houses is in Farndale on the North York Moors. It lies about 14 km north of Kirkbymoorside, on the A170 Thirsk to Scarborough road. There is parking for a handful of cars halfway down a no through road, behind the pub leading to the Daffy Caffy. There is also some parking on the grass verge.

Farndale is noted for its fabulous show of daffodils in springtime.

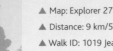

▲ Map: Explorer 27
▲ Distance: 9 km/5½ miles
▲ Walk ID: 1019 Jean Hardman

Difficulty rating

Time

▲ Toilets, Birds, Great Views, Moor, Ancient Monument

The Swastika Stone from Ilkley Town

Ilkley Moor is part of a large area of moorland, known collectively as Rombolds Moor. This walk explores the area around the Swastika Stone, mostly on good tracks and paths.

1 Cross the road and walk up the steps to the paddling pool. Turn left along the path round the pool, then up the steps. Follow the tarmac path to the right of the shelter, then ahead up more steps and along a deeply rutted path towards the house. Take the steps down to the track, which heads downhill. Walk over the bridge and take the path to the left.

2 Follow the path until it comes out on to the road. Turn left up the road for a short distance. At the signpost, turn right and cross over the footbridge. Follow the track along the moorside.

3 Cross the bridge over Black Beck and continue ahead on the path alongside the wall. At the junction bear left away from the wall. Continue on the main path, crossing a series of three stone stiles and one wooden stile, taking in the extensive views across to Wharfedale. Just before the next wooden stile, take the narrow path on the left through the bracken to a stone stile. Go through the stile on to a path over the hill.

4 At the wood, turn left and follow the path, keeping the wood on the right. When you reach the end of the wood, continue up past East Buck Stones, then on to Whetstone Gate.

5 At Whetstone Gate, turn left and follow the wide stony track, passing Cowpers Cross on the left. Continue downhill for about 2 km until the track meets the road.

6 Continue down the road, turn right at the junction and walk back to the car park.

further information

White Wells is a restored 18th-century bathhouse. It is open to visitors most weekends.

access information

There are regular bus and train services from Leeds to Ilkley. If using this form of transport you will need to add an extra 1.5 km to the distance for the walk up Wells Road and back down at the end of the walk.

By car take the A65 to Ilkley. At the traffic lights turn towards the B6382, turn left at the roundabout then first right up Wells Road, over the cattle grid at the top and immediately right into the large car park.

At Ilkley you will see not only the famous moor, but also these magnificent rock formations.

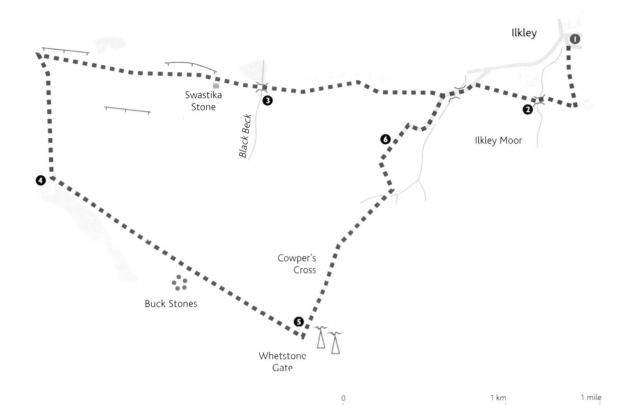

Ilkley

❶

❷

❸ Swastika
Stone

Black Beck

❻

Ilkley Moor

❹

Cowper's
Cross

Buck Stones

❺

Whetstone
Gate

0   1 km   1 mile

*The Swastika Stone is a magnificent
example of a Bronze Age swastika, or
fylfot. The original is on the large boulder,
with a replica nearer the fence.
It is a version of the symbol of eternal life,
and dates from around 1800 BC.*

▲ Map: Explorer OL 10
▲ Distance: 13 km/8 miles
▲ Walk ID: 451 William Kembery

Difficulty rating
❗❗❗

Time
●●●●

▲ Hills or Fells, River, Pub, Toilets, Museum, Play Area, Church, National Trust/NTS, Birds, Flowers, Great Views

Barden Moor above Bolton Abbey

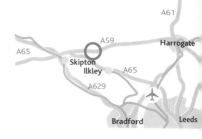

After a pleasant stroll along the Wharfe and a visit to Bolton Priory, the walk crosses the river and climbs up on to the grouse moors, with panoramic views of upper Wharfedale, before returning along the river.

1 Walk towards the river along the old road. Just before the bridge, turn left through a stile. Follow the signs to Bolton Priory.

2 Cross the river by the Priory. Turn left and keep to the lower path. Follow the river to enter the woods by a stile. Continue on this path through the trees. At the lane turn left down the hill to ford the stream. Turn left on to the footpath, signposted Pavilion.

3 Cross the bridge and the road. Head up the track to Bolton Park Farm. Take the left-hand track through a gate at the end of the farm, then across two cattle grids. Follow the track through the moor. At the next junction, take the right fork.

4 At the T-junction, turn right. Follow the track down the valley. Leap over the small ford and continue towards the farm. At the next junction, take the right-hand fork. Keep straight on, following the signs to Storiths. Cross over a stile to reach the next junction.

5 Turn right and continue straight past the farm access road. Keep to this track, leading into Storiths. Cross the road and continue ahead. Take the No Through Road and follow it round a farm to arrive at a gate. Enter the ginnel and walk downhill.

6 At the T-junction, turn left towards Bolton Bridge. Follow this path over two stiles. Turn right and continue to reach

the banks of the river. Cross several fields until you reach a track. Follow the track, climbing left. At the top, keep to the right of the gate to arrive at a stile giving access to a field. Continue on the track and enter the ginnel by a small gate to the right of the farm buildings. At the old road, turn right over the bridge, back to the car.

access information

Parking is off the A59 at Bolton Bridge to the east of Skipton.

Bolton Priory is a 12th-century Augustinian priory near the picturesque village of Bolton Abbey.

Bolton Priory can be visited along the route.
Bardon Moor is an Access Area and may be
closed for some days during the grouse-
shooting season. No dogs are allowed. For
details phone 01756 710533 / 710227

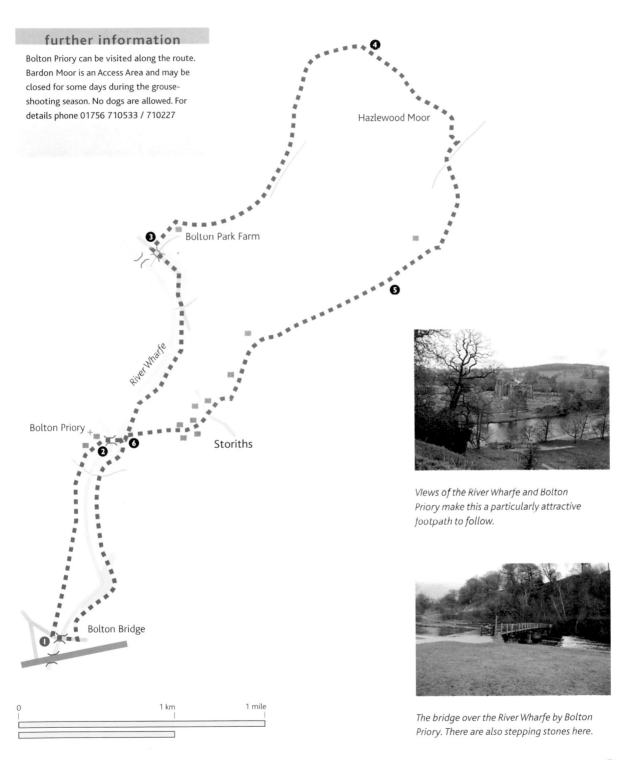

Hazlewood Moor

Bolton Park Farm

River Wharfe

Bolton Priory

Storiths

Bolton Bridge

Views of the River Wharfe and Bolton
Priory make this a particularly attractive
footpath to follow.

The bridge over the River Wharfe by Bolton
Priory. There are also stepping stones here.

0   1 km   1 mile

▲ Map: Explorer 298
▲ Distance: 9 km/5½ miles
▲ Walk ID: 321 Jim Grindle

Difficulty rating

Time

▲ Hills or Fells, River, Lake/Loch,
Pub, Toilets, Museum, Play Area,
Church, Great Views

Guise Cliff from Pateley Bridge

This walk, although relatively short, is wonderfully varied, rising through pastures and moorland, before descending through woods to the riverside. You even pass a very old and unusual folly.

❶ Leave the car park and cross the road. Turn left alongside the playground. Turn left at the junction and then right at Bewerley Farm. Cross the stile and head uphill.

❷ Follow the path to the top of the rise. Go through the stile and continue on the left, to the edge of the wood. Turn left, following the stream downhill, and cross the footbridge. At the lake follow the yellow marker to your right to reach a gravel track and a stile.

❸ Turn right on to the lane. Cross the ford and continue uphill. Follow the lane as it bends left then right, and exit through the gate in the fence. Follow the path along the edge of the wood. Cross the stile and turn left. Go through a gate and turn right. Leave the wood for an open stretch and make for the stone wall. At a large beech tree in the corner, turn to the left and head downhill to a ladder stile. Follow the steep path down to a bridge and up the opposite bank.

❹ Follow the straight track and cross the lane via a kissing gate. Head up the bank by the sign for Guise Cliff. Pass Yorke's Folly and cross the ladder stile. Follow the main track above the cliff top for 1.6 km, crossing numerous stiles on the way.

❺ Go steeply down the track. Follow the path as it winds through the trees and forks left, towards Guisecliff Tarn. After the tarn, turn left. At the next junction take the muddy path to the right. Continue via a stile, steps, an enclosed path and another stile next to a cottage. Continue past the farm to a T-junction. Turn left, and then right to cross the bridge.

❻ Turn left down the gravel track. Pass a reservoir. Just beyond the weir, follow the gravelled riverside path back to the bridge in Pateley.

Brimham Stones, on the moor near Pately Bridge.

Pateley Bridge

①

Bewerley

②

③

④

Yorke's Folly

access information

Pateley Bridge is best reached from the A59 by the B6451. There is a new long-stay car park south of the River Nidd, right by the bridge.

Glasshouses

⑥

Reservoir

Guisecliff Tarn

Guisecliff Wood

Guise Cliff

⑤

0	1 km	1 mile

▲ Map: Explorer 27
▲ Distance: 8.5 km/5¼ miles
▲ Walk ID: 768 Jean Hardman

Difficulty rating

Time

▲ Great Views

Around Chevin Park

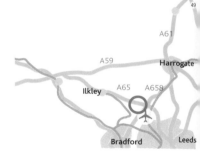

This is a favourite walk for weekend afternoons, with good tracks and superb views to Otley and Wharfedale. If you are lucky, you may spot some of the roe deer that live in Chevin Park – remember to keep dogs under control.

❶ At the car park, go through the gap in the fence. Follow the path, bearing left to reach the main track. Turn right, then take the right fork along the broad track. Cross the stream, and take the right-hand track to the crest of the hill. Continue straight across the junction on a broad, sandy track. At the T-junction turn left, and head downhill. Bear left and go through the kissing gate. At the diverging paths keep straight ahead.

❷ Turn left on to the main track and go through the gate. Follow the broad track to the top of Caley Crags. Continue straight ahead, then cross the bridge. Bear left over the walkway and follow the path on the right.

❸ Take a small path to the right just before the car park, passing through a wooded area, running parallel with the road until you cross a stile. Turn right down the road, keeping to the verge, which becomes a footpath.

❹ Cross the road and enter the East Chevin Quarry car park. At the far end, cross the stile and climb the broad track, which passes through the scrubland and then enters woodland. At the junction turn left. At the top turn right, keeping the woods on the right. Go straight ahead, passing the steps. Pass through a broken wall into a small wooded area. Follow the main path right and go through another broken wall.

❺ Turn left at the junction, following the track uphill. At the top, turn left to reach the main path, and continue straight ahead. Take the next right-hand track, which goes above The Chevin with spectacular views. Continue past a car park.

❻ Turn left at the gate and down the stony track to emerge on East Chevin Road. Cross the road and turn right to reach the car park.

A breathtaking view of Wharfedale on a glorious sunny day.

access information

Chevin Forest Park is south of the A660 Leeds to Otley road. If approaching from Leeds, when you reach the junction with the A658 (traffic lights at Dynley Arms), turn left up the A658 and at the third right-hand junction turn right on to East Chevin Road. The car park is on the right.

Beyond Caley Crags, the path meanders over bridges and through fields and forest.

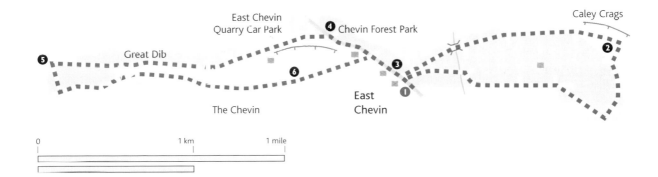

East Chevin
Quarry Car Park

Great Dib

5

Chevin Forest Park **4**

Caley Crags

2

3

The Chevin

East Chevin

6

1

0   1 km   1 mile

▲ Map: Explorer OL 1
▲ Distance: 10 km/6¼ miles
▲ Walk ID: 1137 Barry Smith

Difficulty rating

Time

▲ Hills or Fells, Pub, Toilets, Church, Wildlife, Flowers, Great Views, Moor, Woodland

Pots 'n' Pans from Binns Green

With superb views and plenty of inspiration and opportunities for taking photographs, this walk climbs over moorland then into small hamlets and green lanes for the return.

1 From Binns Green car park, cross the road and take the bridleway opposite, signed Oldham Way. Go to the second stile and turn right. Cross the next stile to start the climb up to the Pots 'n' Pans boulder, which comes into view over the crest of the hill. Follow this track and climb past (or through) the quarry to the summit, where you will come across the boulder with the memorial behind.

2 Go right, through a gap in the iron railings. A stone pillar will confirm you are still on the Oldham Way. Continue on the path ahead, forking left at the marker. Head for the ridge and Shaw Rocks. Looking down, St Chad's Church can be seen. Continue to Slades Rocks.

3 Here, take the lane to the left. After a stile, continue ahead. Pass a left hand fork and follow the next left bend, cross a stile ahead of you and descend into Pobgreen.

4 Bear right and continue on the lane ahead. This soon turns into a path that follows the contours of the hill, crossing three stiles. At the fourth stile bear left, following the marker poles, and cross a broken wall. Keep the poles on your left. Continue by the wall to the corner where the poles meet the wall. Go straight ahead, passing a bench, then bear right slightly downhill.

5 Just before the stile on the right, turn left on to the lane towards Alderman Hill. Just before the farm, take the lane going sharply downhill to your right.

6 You will come out on Long Lane at Yars Hill. Turn left and this will take you to a waymarker. Follow the lane back to Binns Green.

further information

Pots 'n' Pans gets the name from the hollows in the rocks that collect water, said to have healing properties for sore eyes!

Until you follow a footpath such as the Pots 'n' Pans route, it is easy to forget that Britain has some of the most stunning views in the world.

access information

From Oldham, take the A669 to Greenfield. Take the sharp right turn for the rail station and continue sharp left on the A669 to the roundabout. Turn left on the A635 and after 2 km turn right for Binns Green car park. This road also brings you from Holmfirth. The train stops at Greenfield from both sides of the Pennines, and is just 3 km from the start of the walk.

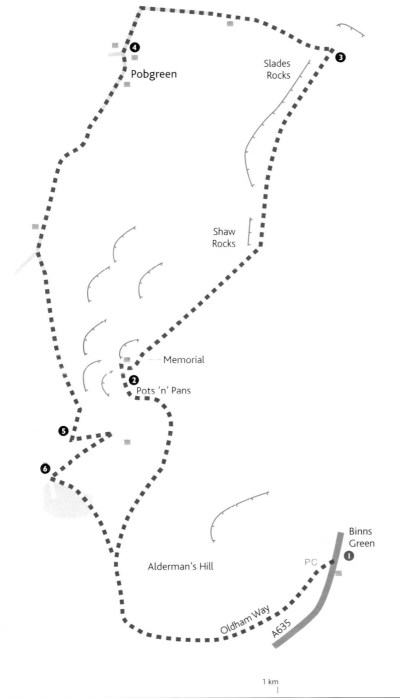

Pobgreen

Slades
Rocks

❸

Shaw
Rocks

Memorial
❷
Pots 'n' Pans

❺

❻

Alderman's Hill

Binns
Green
PC
❶

Oldham Way
A635

0   1 km   1 mile

The Pots 'n' Pans boulder with the
memorial behind.

A stone pillar on the Oldham Way,
just past the Pots 'n' Pans boulder.

Long Lane at Yars Hill, on the return
route to Binns Green.

▲ Map: Explorer OL 21
▲ Distance: 8.86 km/5½ miles
▲ Walk ID: 244 Karen Walton

Difficulty rating

Time

▲ Hills or Fells, Pub, Toilets, Church, Great Views

Barkisland and Greetland from Stainland

This route shows Calderdale at its best, from open views over the surrounding countryside to period houses in local villages, and from hilltop to valley floor via tracks, country lanes and fields.

❶ From the car park turn right into Stainland Road. At the junction bear right, then turn left at the school. When you reach the crossroads, go straight down Coldwells Hill. At a signpost for Sonoco Board Mills, bear right. At a fork bear left over a bridge. Follow the curve of the road, then continue on a sandy track past a farmhouse. Go through a gate into a sloping field. Continue through two fields to a wooden stile.

❷ Turn right up a partly cobbled lane. Continue past Penny Hill Cottage and Park House Farm. Just before a row of houses, turn right. Follow the path into a field, passing through a series of stone stiles.

❸ Turn left into a lane and take the footpath on the right. Cross the field through a stile into a farmyard. Stick to the path through several fields, crossing a brook and a stony lane on the way. Go down the steps, over the beck and up the hill.

❹ Turn left into Stainland Road and pass the Griffin Inn. Turn right into Stoney Butts Lane. Follow the path to the road. Cross the road and continue on the path to Greetland Road. Turn right. Bear right past a farmhouse. Cross a lane and keep forward down a grassy track. At the bottom, turn right and cross Saddleworth Road. Turn left on to a signposted footpath.

❺ Follow the path ahead, turning right then left through a field. Cross the road go through the mill complex. Continue into open fields, following the footpath signposted to Gate Head. Keep close to the brook. Climb the steps and turn right over a bridge. At the lane, bear left and climb the steps, following the sign to Stainland. Follow the yellow markers over the golf course. On reaching a wall, turn right.

❻ At the large boulder, turn left. Then right to follow a walled lane to Stainland Road. Turn right back to the car park.

access information

The walk starts from the village of Stainland, on the B6112 to the west of the A629 between Halifax and Huddersfield. The car park is in the village centre next to the Red Lion. Stainland is easily accessible by bus from Halifax, Elland or Huddersfield.

The hills around Calderdale offer plenty of opportunities to fill your lungs with fresh air.

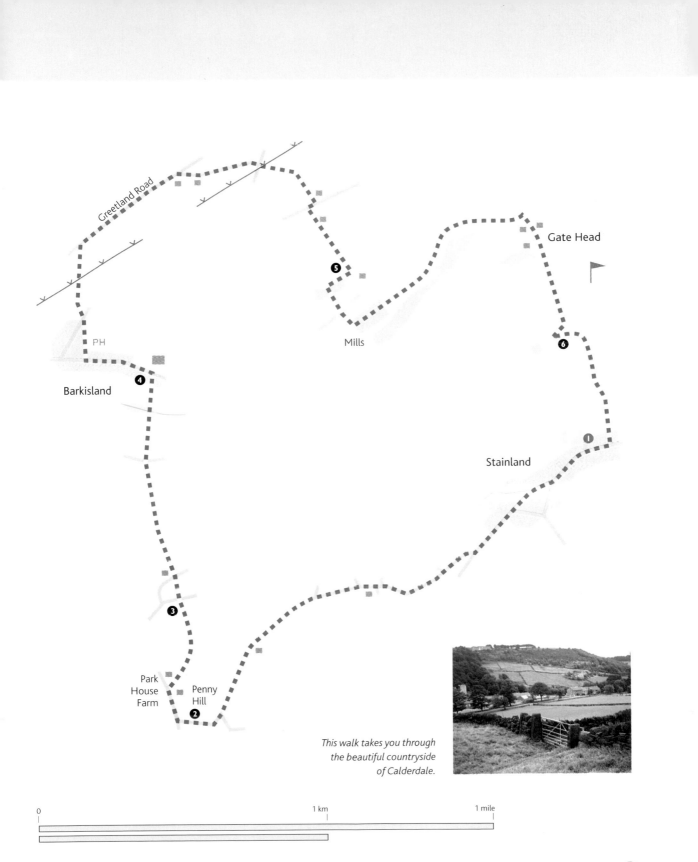

Greetland Road

Gate Head

❺

Mills

❻

PH

Barkisland

❹

Stainland

❶

❸

Park
House
Farm

Penny
Hill

❷

*This walk takes you through
the beautiful countryside
of Calderdale.*

0   1 km   1 mile

Index

acknowledgements

The publishers wish to thank the following for the kind use of their pictures:

COLLECTIONS: pps.22 Graeme Peacock, 60, 62 Lawrence Englesberg CORBIS: pps.13, Kennan Ward, 14 Ric Ergenbright, 18 Julie Meech/Ecoscene, 19 Michael Busselle, 20 Eddie Ryle-Hodges, Sandro Vannini, 30 Michael Busselle, 32/3 Ric Ergenbright, 34 W.A.Sharman, 38 Michael Busselle, 39 Peter Hulme/Ecoscene, 40 Michael Busselle, 40/1 Wildcountry, 44 Patrick Ward, 46 Michael Boys, 49 Michael John Kielty, 50 + 52 Peter M Wilson, 56 Patrick Ward, 60 Sandy Stockwell JULIA EWART: pps.8, 9 JEAN HARDMAN: pps.53, 58 JUDE HOWAT: pps.16, 17, 21, 23, 42, 43, 48 WILLIAM KEMBERY. p.55 both GETTYIMAGES:pps.10/11 Chris Close/The Image Bank, 11 Trevor Wood/Stone, 54 + 58/9 Colin Raw/Stone MICHAEL PARKIN: pps.24, 25, 47 BARRY SMITH: p.61all JOHN THORN: pps.36, 37 KAREN WALTON: p.63